Apocalyptic Polly

A pandemic memoir

By Polly Basore Wenzl

For Henry

There's no big apocalypse.
Just an endless procession
of little ones.
Neil Gaiman

CHAPTER I

Major Life Disruption

The first thing I worried about was water.

It was February 25, 2020. As I drove home from work, a woman on the radio — someone with the Centers for Disease Control and Prevention — was warning of a coming global pandemic that would soon bring "major life disruption." She was warning people to prepare for everything about our normal lives to change.

What did that mean? What could that possibly mean?

I grew up in the 1970s and early 1980s in a ranch-style house in Oklahoma, chosen by my mother for the basement because of her fear of tornadoes. But the basement wasn't built for tornadoes. It was built as a bomb shelter — a nuclear bomb shelter. We rarely went down there except when tornado sirens blew.

It was a dank, poorly lit, musty place with spiders, furnished with two twin beds propped on palettes because the basement flooded regularly. It was never explained to me why there were beds in a place no one would ever want to sleep. It was also stocked with board games and gallons of water stored in old milk jugs.

None of this made sense to me as a child and no adult explained it. Not until I more fully understood the Cold War and the grim purpose of a bomb shelter — to wait out the nuclear winter ash and radiation after-effects of a nuclear blast. Preparation for a slim chance of survival.

My parents knew something about the need for survival. Both had been born in the 1920s, before most vaccines and antibiotics. My mother was quarantined and bed-ridden for months as a child with diphtheria, so long that she had to learn to walk again at the age of 8. Both Mom and Dad had been children during the Depression, luckier than most because their parents held jobs, but all too aware of scarcity and famine and people who lacked for the most basic needs, including as my mom often recalled, children who went without shoes in the winter.

They came of age during World War II, and my father did his service fighting the Japanese on a submarine in the South Pacific, an experience he described as hours and hours of boredom, punctuated by moments of sheer terror when depth charges shook the sub. They survived all this only to see their adult years defined by the Cold War and threats of nuclear annihilation.

The Cold War lasted from 1947 to 1991, when two World War II allies — the United States and the Soviet Union — emerged as the dominating superpowers and began vying for control of the globe. Both amassed tremendous military might, including nuclear weapons, which they threatened to use against each other. They avoided direct confrontation, often fighting proxy wars instead (the Korean War, the Vietnam War). Instead the rivals maintained a fragile peace built on the idea that if they ever did use their nukes against each other, the result would so horribly cataclysmic neither side would survive.

Such a war wouldn't only bring massive instant death from the blasts, but widespread slow death from radiation poisoning and starvation as the nuclear fallout — radioactive ash — destroyed plants and animals. My father spent a good portion of his professional life trying to prevent such a thing. Dad also worried about looming threats brought on by carbon energy use and global population growth. He predicted food shortages, energy shortages, and resultant widespread starvation and war. I grew up aware of all these bad things that might one day happen. Not because my parents meant to scare me but because they were determined to prepare and prevent, in whatever means was in their power to do so.

It all seemed so distant, so unreal, so hypothetical, growing up in the 1970s and 1980s. I grew up upper middle class in a university town on a sunny street in a neighborhood where almost everyone had a parent with a PhD, full of kids who rode bicycles and played outside. I had not known a war in my lifetime other than Vietnam, which I was too young to remember. We lacked for nothing at home. Christmas and birthdays were celebrated with lots of presents. We were healthy, and while certainly not always happy, I never remember feeling unsafe. My parents were protecting me. My sense of safety emboldened me to take risks — riding in the back of pickups, climbing fire towers, jumping off railroad bridges as a teen, then going off as a young woman alone to explore big cities as a young adult.

Which is to say nothing really prepared me for what was to come. When I walked in the door after arriving home that night in February 2020, my first thoughts went to water. I asked my husband if we shouldn't immediately clean out the basement and stock gallons of water. He looked at me blankly. Our problem wasn't going to be water, he said.

Both my husband, Roy, a retired journalist, and my son, Henry, a graduate student in physics, had taken the threat of the pandemic more seriously. My son started talking about it in December 2019, warning me of the virus spreading through China that threatened to spread across the world.

Apocalyptic Polly

Henry was an insatiable consumer of news and current events, and had a particular interest in China, having studied Chinese three years in high school and visited Beijing in 2012. He had moved in with us to save money while attending graduate school. I dismissed his worries and told him of all the things I worried about, a global pandemic didn't even make the list.

My husband began expressing real concern after the city of Wuhan went on lockdown on January 23, 2020. I didn't know anything about Wuhan and wasn't sure what "lockdown" even meant. I suggested the media, to get clicks, was perhaps making too much of it. Roy got irritated with me for being dismissive, and rightly pointed out the serious implications of locking down a city of 19 million — ordering people to stay in their homes and not to leave for work, school, or even to shop for anything but food.

I didn't have room in my brain for this, couldn't begin to process what any of this meant. *How can people live if they can't leave home? How do they eat? How do the children learn? How do people do their jobs and earn money to pay their bills?* Impossible. Unthinkable. So I didn't think about it, until I had to, when that woman on the radio said "major life disruption" was coming to America.

The first public health messaging was about handwashing, and the first sign that things were off was the scarcity of hand sanitizer.

We began seeing public service messages everywhere telling us the importance of regular and thorough handwashing. NPR aired a story about songs you could sing to measure out the 20 seconds necessary for a thorough handwashing. *"Happy Birthday to you ... "* Alternatively, we were told when handwashing wasn't possible to use hand sanitizer, that goopy alcohol-based gel that somehow goes dry when you rub it into your hands long enough, leaving them smelling like vodka.

By the time I thought to go buy hand sanitizer I found store shelves empty. I checked the grocery store, two pharmacies, a Walmart. Nothing. Just empty shelves where the hand sanitizer was supposed to be, along with signs telling shoppers to take no more than two per customer.

My parents had lived through World War II with its ration books that limited the amount of sugar, coffee, meat, cheese, and canned goods you could buy. My only previous experience with scarcity was in the Soviet Union. The Cold War had loomed so large in my life, I had studied journalism and Russian language in college. I was working in Moscow as a journalist in the summer of 1991, immediately before the collapse of the Soviet Union that ended the Cold War. I cut my stay short and came home because I could not deal with the hunger brought on by the profound scarcity of empty store shelves, bread lines, and the daily hunt for food to eat. The Soviet Union was on the brink of economic collapse — having overspent on its military and weapons — and failed to function in the most basic ways. I came home appreciating for the first time just how functional the United States was. Except for Cabbage Patch dolls and Wii gaming systems, I had never encountered scarcity at home — until now.

My older sister, who had been paying closer attention to all of this, suggested I go to Bath & Body Works, a specialty retailer known for selling things that smell nice: soaps, candles, lotions, and I soon learned, hand sanitizer. A 34-ounce bottle of hand sanitizer cost about $5 at Walmart. Bath & Body Works sold its hand-sanitizer in tiny 1-ounce bottles for about $1.50 each — more than 10 times as expensive.

In my first act of pandemic-fueled hoarding, I bought a dozen of the little bottles. They were strangely cheerful, containing brightly colored gel speckled with glitter, in scents that smelled of beach drinks. The store also sold a dazzling array of trinkets to attach said hand sanitizer to your purse. All of it ironically made in China. In an act of black comedy, I bought a fuzzy rabbit's head sanitizer dispenser, attached it to my purse and called it "Pandemic Bunny." I thought this was very funny, but no one else ever laughed.

My sister and I urgently wanted hand sanitizer because we were planning to meet up the first week of March in Atlanta for her granddaughter's 5th birthday, me flying in from Kansas and my sister from Hawaii.

Raised as we were in a family of government scientists, including a grandmother who worked in public health during the 1918 Spanish Flu, my sister and I paid close attention to every advisory coming from the CDC. We thought we were safe to fly, until the CDC announced, after we both left, that the elderly and the medically vulnerable should avoid air travel.

At that time, most advisories focused on how surfaces could be contaminated with virus. *Wash your hands, don't touch your face.* The fear was the virus could migrate from a contaminated surface to your hands, to your eyes, nose, or mouth. So, we compared notes and agreed to both stock up on hand sanitizer and Clorox wipes and touch as little as possible while traveling. What we did touch, we would wipe down with Clorox wipes first: our IDs for airport security, our airplane seats, our hotel keys and hotel nightstands, our phones.

When we arrived in Atlanta, our cautionary fervor caught my niece Melody off guard. A young professional woman raising two young children, she didn't have much time for scouring news and public health websites. Mentally, she seemed to be where I was a few weeks prior: vaguely aware of a pandemic threat but wholly unprepared for the radical change it might bring to her life.

When I suggested that her children's daycare might close and asked whether she could work from home, she looked at me with a combination of disbelief and anger — exactly the reaction countless working parents would have when confronted with the total life upheaval that could bring.

Eventually her mother and I wore her down, urging Melody to

take this seriously and at least start using hand sanitizer on herself and her kids. I suggested we go to Bath & Body Works. That was unnecessary, she said, as she pulled out her phone to order some hand sanitizer off Amazon.com, where until this point in time virtually any consumer product could be bought with a single click and delivered the next day. I watched Melody's face form a scowl. *"It's sold out. How can it be sold out?!"*

I gave Melody a few of my tiny bottles and suggested we go to Bath & Body Works for more. She was still incredulous. We went to Walmart first because it was closer. By now stores were familiar with the public's demand for hand sanitizer and surface disinfectants and had set up special displays with everything in one place, like those at Thanksgiving offering ingredients for stuffing, green bean casserole, pumpkin pie, and cranberries.

A clerk pointed us to an area of the store where the disinfecting products were displayed but cautioned us: *"We've been sold out for about a week."* We turned a corner to see an entire aisle of empty shelves where the hand sanitizer, Clorox wipes, and 409 spray had been. Melody looked shocked. My sister and I were no longer, and I suggested again that we make a trek across town to the Bath & Body Works.

It was at least a 20-minute drive through Atlanta traffic. When we finally got there, I rushed to the part of the store I expected the hand sanitizer to be. Nothing but empty bins. A store clerk grimly told us they had been sold out for two weeks. But then something miraculous occurred — a UPS driver walked in with a new shipment! At least a half-dozen people in the store immediately lined up behind the store worker opening the boxes and refilling the bins. *No more than six to a customer.* We were limited to six 1-ounce bottles, less than the amount in an ordinary bottle of hand sanitizer. The three of us each bought the max so Melody would have what we thought was enough.

Later that day, when Melody went to pick up her 2-year-old son from daycare, she suddenly noticed all the things she needed to touch to do so. The door to get in, the gate to access the children's area, the pen to sign out her child. I could see on her face her mind working, putting it all together, the risks of being in public that she had never considered. She used hand sanitizer afterward.

But we had not come for a pandemic drill session. We were there for a 5-year-old girl's birthday party. It was held in a neighborhood park, where children could climb and swing on playground equipment before cake and punch at picnic tables. And what happened next was exactly what would play out across America through the year to come.

"Hand sanitizer? Why do you need hand sanitizer? Kids need to be exposed to germs so they can build up their immune systems," the other grandmother said dismissively to my sister. And so it began: The division of families by disagreement over the risks posed by Covid-19 and what to do about them.

My father came back from World War II with a particular set of skills and mindset. A radar man in the Navy, he became an amateur radio operator. Hams, as they were called, were hobbyists who used amateur radio to manage emergency communications around the world. In 1952, they formally became affiliated with Civil Defense, a public engagement effort intended to respond to natural disasters but also to prepare for potential nuclear catastrophe. The tenets of civil defense: *prepare, prevent, and respond.*

What this looked like to me as a child: I had a father who was frequently present at large public events, wearing an orange vest, talking into a hand-held radio, and directing people as to what to do. What this meant to me as an adult: I thought such behavior was completely normal and adopted it myself. See a potential danger?

Prepare, prevent, and respond. And what it looked like to my first husband, Brett? Paranoia. His nickname for me was "Apocalyptic Polly." I was always forecasting potential dangers and dictating what steps we should take to protect ourselves.

All of which is to say that before I got home from Atlanta, I had already determined to cancel everything. Immediately.

> ### Facebook: March 9, 2020
> *Everyone still attending conferences and games and going to movies and large public gatherings must not be reading the news. If you have immunity problems, underlying health problems or are over 60 you really need to take this shit seriously.*

When I posted this, I immediately got pushback from friends who were doing exactly these things or planning upcoming events and workshops that contributed to their livelihoods. The reaction made me so uncomfortable I took down the post. How, I wondered, do you urge people to protect themselves against a threat that doesn't yet seem real to them, when the very real need to support themselves is top of mind?

My job also included event planning. My 15-year journalism career had ended some time ago with the contraction of the news industry. I now worked in outreach and recruitment at the local public university. A major part of my job involved running engineering summer camps attended by hundreds of children and teens. More immediately, I was overseeing a career day event, scheduled for the end of March, that would bring hundreds of high school students and dozens of industry professionals to campus, to intermingle in small conference rooms.

On my first day back to work after Atlanta, I assembled my fellow event organizers and made the case to cancel the event. *"Do you really want to be first?"* a colleague asked. No one else on campus had canceled anything yet. Public events are the lifeblood of campus recruitment. It was March 11, 2020, the same day the World Health Organization officially declared a global pandemic. I did not hesitate to be first.

After the meeting, I went to my office, sent out emails to everyone effected notifying them of the cancellation, then packed up my work laptop and all the papers I would need, and did not ask but simply told my bosses I would be working at home. I did not return for 453 days. ❖

CHAPTER **2**

Not Remotely Prepared

The day after Christmas 2004, a 9.1-magnitude undersea earthquake in the Indian Ocean caused the waters to withdraw from the shoreline in Indonesia. Curious people walked onto dry beaches to observe abandoned fish flapping in the sand. Confusion over this unprecedented occurrence caught people off-guard. Hours passed between the earthquake and the tsunami that returned the waters with a vengeance, ultimately killing 228,000 people in one of the deadliest natural disasters in history. That would be a mere fraction of the people ultimately killed in 2020 by Covid-19, but in mid-March that year it seemed we were like curious, confused people wandering the beach.

Change came like a torrent. The day after I moved home to work, our university president announced that students were not to return to campus from spring break. Instead, break would be extended a week to give faculty a chance to prepare to teach classes remotely. A few days after that, the governor of Kansas closed all public schools, directing school districts to implement distance learning. And a week after that, most of the nation went into lockdown, everyone but "essential workers" being told to stay home. Shock, turmoil, anger, resentment, and fear ensued.

My immediate household was far more fortunate than most. My husband was already retired. I was able to work from home. My son, Henry, the graduate student, was probably hit the hardest. In his first semester as a graduate teaching assistant, he was responsible for teaching three sections of physics labs. How would he teach a hands-on physics lab remotely? Online lab simulations, apparently. Roy, a writer, surrendered his desk in our basement office for Henry to use for school. Roy instead took up residence at the dining table, while I moved into the basement office at a desk across from my son.

We all downloaded a video conferencing app called Zoom and tried to adapt to social interactions limited to looking at people in little rectangles sitting in front of their own video screens. Because Zoom allowed people to turn off their cameras and microphones, you would frequently find yourself staring at black boxes with names on them. A great feature for someone trying to multitask during a meeting; horrendous for anyone attempting to gauge student comprehension while teaching.

Parents of young children complained bitterly. How were they supposed to work jobs from home while simultaneously corralling restless children for remote schooling? What if their jobs did not permit them to work from home? Who would watch the kids? Or alternatively, who would pay the bills if they quit to stay home?

My stepdaughter found it all but impossible to engage our special needs, developmentally delayed twin granddaughters in remote learning. Her daughter in high school became depressed from the social isolation of doing school from a laptop in her bedroom. No more choir, band, drama classes with friends. My niece Melody was relieved to be permitted to do her job remotely — but soon found it much harder to provide counseling to troubled kids via video conferencing rather than visit them at school, as she normally did.

But we at least had incomes.

According to the U.S. Bureau of Labor Statistics, the scale of job loss had no precedent since the end of World War II. More than twice as many jobs were lost between March and April 2020 than during the entire recession of the late 2000s — a time of utter financial devastation for many, including me, who went bankrupt.

One in four Americans reported someone in their household was laid off or lost their job. Mass layoffs occurred when restaurants and retail businesses suddenly had no customers because everyone was staying home. This rippled out to affect other industries that produced products no one was buying. Universities like mine feared loss of enrollment. The initial shock caused the stock market to crater, losing 30 percent of its value. (It recovered a few months later.)

Government tried to help with the $2.2 trillion Coronavirus Aid, Relief, and Economic Security (CARES) Act, the largest government economic stimulus program in U.S. history. The CARES Act passed Congress quickly, with overwhelming bipartisan support. It provided direct cash payments to most Americans, increased unemployment benefits, and subsidized loans to small businesses meant to help them keep staff on payroll. It also infused local and state governments, universities, and other institutions with cash to offset pandemic-related costs.

It was not enough to blunt the impact of layoffs, however. Outdated government computer systems were overwhelmed and people who needed those unemployment benefits waited months to get their applications approved. Moratoriums on evictions helped people stay in their homes but strained property owners who then couldn't pay their own bills.

It soon became clear to me that following public health guidelines was a privilege not everyone had. People fighting for daily economic survival angrily resented the shutdowns and dismissed as fear-mongering the public health warnings about what might happen to the estimated 1 percent who might die from Covid-19, even if that percent added up to hundreds of thousands of people.

On March 19, I wrote the first of several pandemic diary entries I shared on Facebook. This one focused on how grocery shopping had become a surreal experience.

Apocalyptic Polly

Facebook: Pandemic Diary, March, 19, 2020

At the Dillons grocery store at 13th and West, there were five people waiting outside the door at 5:55 a.m., several more in cars, including me. The relative crowd surprised me given the hour, the thunderstorm, and the fact it was the day before payday. I waited for the door to open and the "crowd" to thin before going in. The saniwipe container was empty, so I slathered on my fragrant and glittery Bath and Body Works hand sanitizer and slid my hands across the cart push bar.

Once inside, I turned right, as I always have, toward produce. Plenty of bananas today when I didn't need any. I grabbed some bagged salads. The produce section and deli were deserted, and I soon realized everyone else had headed straight for the toilet paper. By the time I got there, a small stack remained. The limit said three per customer. I took two. When I made it to the bakery, I overheard a group of store workers talking. One told the others, "Everything is off. No more restrictions on over-time." Another replied, "Are you sure? Just yesterday John was telling me, 'Clock out! It's time to clock out!'" The first one insisted, no more restrictions on working overtime.

By the time I made it to meats, where most of the hamburger was gone but plenty of steaks remained, I heard a young woman — late 20s, early 30s — telling a couple of stockers that she had just been laid off. She looked shell-shocked. Her basket held just a few items. The stockers told her excitedly, "Apply at a grocery store! We're hiring!"

Even at 6:05 a.m., the aisles seemed crowded, not with people but with pallets of food being restocked. Shoppers avoided each other as best they could, but with the pallets, it was challenging. Except for the laid off woman, all the shoppers were over 50 like me.

I managed to find everything on my list, except Clorox wipes and whole milk. When I was ready to check out, I noticed only self-service was open. An older (than me) woman saw my full cart and motioned to a coworker, a man who I took to be in his early 70s, to open a lane and check me out. While he was scanning and bagging my groceries, I couldn't help but say to him, "I really appreciate you for being here." He stopped and smiled at me, "I really appreciate you for giving me a paycheck."

The groceries rung up to way more than I expected, and I had to stop and check my bank balance and move cash from savings to cover it. Because as I said, it is the day before payday.

I loaded my groceries bags into the trunk in the rain, came home, wiped each item with a Clorox wipe before putting it away, then took a shower and put all my clothes in the washing machine, because some expert said I should do that.

In late March 2020, a Michigan doctor posted a video suggesting people keep the virus out of their homes by following procedures used by surgeons to keep medical instruments sterile. The video quickly went viral, viewed more than 24 million times in the first week. The steps he described were extreme and overwhelming, and millions of us started doing all of it, while the rest thought we were nuts:

- Wipe down the entire shopping cart with an antiseptic wipe.
- Only touch items you intend to buy.
- Stay 6 feet away from other shoppers, and don't shop in person at all if you or someone in your household is medically vulnerable.
- When you bring groceries home, leave nonperishables outside in a garage or porch for three days. (Covid-19 was not believed to live on surfaces more than 72 hours.)
- For handling groceries brought into your home, prepare a surface with a dirty side and a sterile side, cleaned with disinfectant.
- Place grocery bags on the dirty side. Wipe each packaged item with a Clorox wipe or a rag saturated with disinfectant and then place on the sterile side before putting away.
- Fresh fruits and vegetables should be hand-washed with soapy water, but not with disinfectant. (I got sick after doing this one — and surely so did a lot of people, as the doctor later posted a follow-up video revising his advice to rinsing produce with cold running water.)
- Takeout food should be removed from all containers, which should be immediately discarded, and placed on clean plates before serving. Hands should be washed thoroughly between handling and serving the food.

Apocalyptic Polly

Why would I do all this? Because I honestly believed I was protecting my family from a deadly disease that could kill them. I did it every time I got groceries for over a year, and every time we got takeout. I did it with the same practiced determination I'd seen my parents show whenever a tornado warning was issued: Find the candles and matches (so you could see when the power went out), put fresh batteries in the transistor radios (so you would be alerted to emergency warnings), crack the windows to even out the house's air pressure (so the windows wouldn't break in the event of a sudden barometric pressure drop), and put the shoes by the door (should evacuation become necessary and you might be walking on broken glass and splintered wood.). Not all these tornado precautions were necessary or wise, any more than the doctor's video recommendations. People do what they think is necessary to keep their families safe, but often don't agree about what that is. And as people learn more, so-called "best practices" change, often much faster than our practiced behaviors do. And some people, we learned, expect authority to get it right the first time, not keep changing directives.

———————————— ▭ ————————————

When Roy first told me about the Wuhan lockdown, my first concern was figuring out how people survived under such circumstances. I learned not everyone was really required to stay home. People could leave to perform "essential functions" such as buying and selling food and medications and home repair goods. This created a new economy in which people who stayed home could rely on other people to deliver things to them. It worked in China, and it would work here in America.

Early on our family decided to stay home in isolation, even once the strict lockdown was lifted. We did this in part because we could but also because I felt that my husband at 65, overweight and with a history of heart problems, was at high risk of dying from Covid-19. Public health officials were asking people to stay home as much as possible. I was surprised at how a life that once seemed unthinkable quickly became routine.

I downloaded two apps to my phone: Instacart and DoorDash. Instacart allowed me to order my groceries and have them delivered to my doorstep hours later. DoorDash allowed me to have restaurant meals delivered within an hour. The convenience added roughly 30% to 40% to the cost, but it seemed more than worth it every time a delivery person — many of whom had been laid off from other jobs — thanked me for providing them an income. I tipped generously and put a sign in the front window that said, "Thank You," and featured colorful drawings of delivery people — Postal carriers, UPS and FedEx delivery drivers, and grocery and restaurant delivery service people. Several times I saw people photographing the sign and smiling as they walked away from our house.

The Atlantic Monthly suggested there might be something wrong in what I was doing. The magazine ran an article in April 2020 titled: "*Is It Ethically Okay to Get Food Delivered Right Now? A guide to this and other pandemic food dilemmas.*" The author of the piece rightly noted that food delivery allowed the privileged to stay home while the economically challenged risked their health and well-being for our convenience. It occurred to me how privileged one must be to ponder the ethics of their choices — you can't do that unless you have choices. The ethicists interviewed concluded that delivery reduced interactions between people overall and therefore contributed to reduced community health risk. The people doing delivery were going to face essentially the same health risks whether you ordered delivery or not but would at least have the benefit of an income they might not otherwise have.

Delivery services were all that kept most restaurants in business, but that only provided work for cooks and a few staff. Waiters and bartenders were laid off. In contrast, grocery stores saw their revenues boosted by panic bulk-buying, as people sought to minimize their trips out and ensure they never ran out of staples.

Anytime I could get toilet paper I felt lucky. It was rationed to one or two packages a person. Clorox wipes were also hard to come by. Fearing a milk shortage, I bought dry milk and shelf-stable milk in bulk. A milk shortage never materialized and most of my supply expired before I used it. I also bought a huge amount of dry Gatorade mix because someone advised we should have it on hand if a family member got sick. *Prevent, prepare, respond.*

According to Wikipedia, the principle of people physically separating to reduce the spread of the disease dates to 5th century B.C. One of the earliest known references to the practice is in the Bible, Leviticus 13:46: "And the leper in whom the plague is ... he shall dwell alone; [outside] the camp shall his habitation be."

But according to Merriam-Webster, the term "social distancing" wasn't introduced until the 21st century during the public health response to SARS (Severe Acute Respiratory Syndrome) in 2003. By the end of March 2020, "social distancing" was an all-too-familiar buzz phrase that meant to stay at least 6 feet away from people you didn't live with to prevent the spread of disease.

Staying at home made this simple. But in public spaces, people were soon greeted with lines of tape on the floor marking out 6-foot distances, intended to keep everyone separated in store checkout lines and other places of congregation. A painful subtext to social distancing was the end of physical contact: no hugging your friends and family, no handshaking. People began bumping elbows as a greeting.

But even as we were forced to become physically distant, a weird intimacy arose from the sudden reconfiguration of our lives:

Facebook: March 31, 2020

Me: *Have you noticed that while we are socially distancing, we are getting up in each other's lives a bit more with these Zoom meetings connecting people's homes? For example, while I work at home, my son is taking his classes across the table from me, allowing me to eavesdrop his advanced math and physics lectures, including the interruptions by his instructors' children. He in turn has been an off-camera participant in my office meetings. Interesting dynamic for sure.*

M——: *And you get to see into everyone's homes. I've been doing yoga classes via Zoom and a number of people in class roll out their mats in their bedrooms. (We have our cameras on.) It's a much more intimate peek into people's lives than we've had before in some ways.*

S——: *Yes, I find myself answering (my son)'s biology class questions. He's in the dining room, and I'm in the kitchen.*

M——: *Definitely interesting trying to have a "confidential" therapy session with kids and then my own kids screaming and then me yelling at them.*

L——: *My hubby works from home all the time, so hearing his conference calls are an everyday event. I probably know more about Continuous Process Improvement than most people.*

E——: *Yes! (My boss) asked me today to clarify whether I was actually working in a closet. Lol I've just set my office up in a bedroom that I use as a large closet.*

The intrusion on privacy created by Zoom meetings prompted public debates about whether students doing "distance learning" should be required to keep their cameras on. Many experts said no, not just because of the privacy invasion but because many households did not have the Wi-Fi bandwidth to support constant video feeds — much less multiple feeds in households where two parents and more than one child might simultaneously be online.

Necessity being the mother of invention, Zoom users with enough bandwidth were soon taking advantage of "Zoom backgrounds." Much like the green screen technology that has long allowed TV weather forecasters to stand in front of weather maps, Zoom backgrounds allowed people to mask the actual scene behind them with any image of their choosing. I first noticed this in use when a Harry Potter fan work colleague of mine appeared to be inside Hogwarts.

But this solution didn't work for everyone. Only the fastest computers with the strongest signal bandwidth could use this feature. Others simply turned their cameras off. Socially distanced, we became a nation of disembodied souls trapped in black boxes. ❖

CHAPTER 3

There's No Place But Home

Staying at home allowed me to rebuild my relationship with my cats.

Mr. Boots, a tuxedo short hair, and Noel, a white cat resembling a small polar bear, for years had been my constant companions — and often my only companions — through difficult periods of recession, an attempt at self-employment that ended in bankruptcy, and empty-nest syndrome when my son went off to college. The cats kept my house from feeling empty. They were always either at my side or lounging in the front window staring out at the world.

When I married in 2016, my husband insisted the cats live outdoors. It was a hard adjustment for me, but the cats seemed to thrive. They became more active, their coats lusher and shinier, their lives imbued with new adventures involving birds and squirrels, possums, and raccoons. Like my college-aged son, they developed their own lives apart from me. In my post-marriage, pre-pandemic life, I would take five minutes in the morning to feed them before rushing off to work. I would see them again briefly in the evening, as they stood outside the dining room window watching us eat.

Just as my relationship with them changed when the cats moved outside, it would change again when the pandemic moved my own life outdoors.

Apocalyptic Polly

The backyard became my refuge. A safe, privacy-fenced space where I would sit hours at a time seeking the peace nature provided, along with the comforting presence of Mr. Boots and Noel. Every day we would spend time together, sitting in a wicker chair under the shade of a 200-year-old oak tree.

It was a peaceful world. A variety of flowers bloomed in cycle with the seasons — iris then peony, coneflowers then sunflowers — drawing bees and butterflies. We hung bird feeders, then squirrel-proof feeders, which attracted cardinals, blue jays, woodpeckers, wrens, and finches — and more squirrels. The natural world of the backyard had a predictable rhythm to it that provided a calm the outside world was destroying.

That outside world found its way into my head primarily through social media, through constant updates of the rising counts of Covid-19 infections and deaths, reminders of escalating threat levels and declining hospital capacity, and the escalating anger between those worried primarily for their health and others scared for their livelihoods. Many people, of course, worried about both. We should have been pulling together, but everyone was pulling apart.

Perhaps I should have stayed offline; many people deleted the Facebook app off their phones to stay sane. In lockdown — much as before — Facebook was my primary source of social connection, linking me to distant friends who'd shared my past, family spread around the country, and others in my local community I could no longer see in person. I frequently turned to them for support.

Facebook: April 1, 2020

Me: *I woke up feeling my fear-level has subsided from "my toddler is in a burning car, and I must get him out" to "I need something from the scary dark basement, but the light's burned out." Is this what Pink Floyd meant by "comfortably numb"? What's your metaphor for your anxiety level?*

Facebook: April 1, 2020 *(cont.)*

L—: *Totally agree. It will be interesting to see how we all behave as time moves forward. I recall reading a story — I think in Malcolm Gladwell's book, Outliers — regarding the English during bombings by the Germans and how the English government was preparing a lot of mental institutions because the popular thought was the public might completely fall apart mentally from all the bombing/stress. And much to their surprise, the English citizens became sort of numb and carried on their normal lives despite the craziness around them.*

Me: *Right. We need to find the bearable middle ground between vigilance and hyper-vigilance.*

K—: *I had a complete utter meltdown yesterday over a plant. They announced our office is closed through April. I asked if there was a way to go retrieve my plant. They considered my request, but ultimately said no. I cried uncontrollably for about 10 minutes. (I know it's not the plant.)*

L—: *My life took such an unexpected left turn (with cancer) last year, that I'm just kind of "meh" about this new craziness. I'm at the point where I think we are all going to get Covid eventually. Do I like that thought? Absolutely not. But I went through all the stages of grief in November and December, and I don't have the energy to do it again.*

R—: *I feel like I am living in a bubble. Limited physical contact, no happy hour, no coffee talk with friends, working from home, worrying I am breathing Covid aerosol whenever I am within 6' of someone ...*

Peggy: *The threat from the virus feels like this: I am locked in a room where it is generally quiet and safe. I don't hate the room because it keeps me healthy. But if I open the door a crack, for even a second, I hear the collective gasping for breath of all the people who are dying of covid-19, and the screams of futility from the medical personnel who don't have what they need to arm themselves for this war. It's terrifying, so I have to close the door again, knowing that the only thing I can do to help any of those people is to stay in this room.*

Me: *Exactly*

L—: *Geez you really nailed that for me too.*

B—: *I grew up in a family dominated by a violent alcoholic father. Covid-19 fears are a walk in the park.*

Facebook: Pandemic Diary, April 17, 2020

What day is it? What month? What year? That my mind halted over simply writing the date is a good indicator of where I am.

Instacart just delivered our groceries for the week. My husband noticed the delivery person did not wear a mask. I wiped every grocery item down thoroughly, but still tipped her $20 and felt like it wasn't enough.

I am lucky to still have a job, though I have much less to do than usual right now, because the 18 summer camps I normally run are canceled. I am told a likely furlough and possible layoff is in the near future. It is hard to sleep at night when you are constantly on high alert for threats to your well-being. I rarely sleep more than an hour at a time overnight. This feeling can make you overlook how many things are good. So I manage to feel guilty about that, too.

Higher ed is starting to look like the newspaper industry in terms of its future. Not good. If students don't return in adequate numbers in the fall, many of us will lose our jobs. But if students do return to campus and it's not really safe, how many of us might lose our lives?

Even if I get laid off, my son would still have to go back to take classes and teach classes — interacting with 100 different people or more during the week and then coming home. How will the university possibly create the social-distancing and sanitation necessary to make that safe? Even if we re-open, who is to say the students will come? Can you really blame a parent who wouldn't want to send their first-time freshman off to college in the middle of this?

And I know this higher ed thing is just one tiny slivered, privileged problem to have, when there is so much hurting and loss and poverty and disease and loneliness out there.

I'm going to go check on my cats now.

Anxiety and depression became their own epidemic during the pandemic with 40% of people reporting symptoms during 2020 — nearly four times as many as in 2019, according to the CDC. There was plenty to be afraid of and depressed about: the looming threat of a deadly disease, imposed lockdowns that separated families, the economic impact of so many people losing jobs, and increasing social and political upheaval. Each day felt like a fight to survive, physically and mentally.

Strangely, my family history of mental illness seemed to serve me. My mother had suffered agoraphobia — a fear of going out in public that triggered panic attacks. My father showed signs of obsessive-compulsive disorder. I inherited mild versions of both, while my son developed full-blown OCD.

What was generally a curse suddenly seemed a blessing. I knew, for example, I would never have to worry about my son touching an infected door handle, gas pump, or other public surface. He had already spent years touching as little as possible and using hand sanitizer generously. And agoraphobia? I leaned in. There had never been a better time to be a person with no desire to leave home. I was content to be homebound with the two people I loved most.

At least that's what I told myself. Truth was, the pandemic's impact on mental health was devastating, and looking back I wonder how many decisions I made trying to protect my family ended up harming them. Increasingly consumed by fear, I constantly questioned my own judgment.

We all felt it. I got so I wouldn't answer the door, not for strangers, neighbors, or friends, for fear of letting the virus in my home. I got agitated and berated my husband after he opened the door to speak to a neighbor kid about retrieving a ball that had gone over our fence. Not allowing anyone in our home meant no more housekeepers, no more repairmen (with one exception for a plumbing emergency), no friends, and no family.

Before the pandemic, my husband paid almost daily visits to his daughter's house to play with our developmentally disabled granddaughters who thrived on his attention. His absence was heartbreaking for him and the girls, but we all deemed the separation necessary to protect everyone's health. He also stopped visiting his elderly mother, in her 80s.

My son similarly saw little of his father, Brett, who lived three hours away in Tulsa. Normally, Henry might go stay with his dad for a few days every few months. I proposed that maybe Henry could visit his dad if either his dad's family strictly isolated at home for 14 days beforehand, or Henry isolated within our home for 14 days following a visit. (Fourteen days was the length of time believed for Covid-19 to run its course and no longer be infectious, according to the CDC.) Brett didn't want to do that, because his grandson Landon, 8, was living with him and seeing friends, a decision made to support the child's mental health. But Brett also didn't want to risk infecting Roy, so he stayed away.

Text to Brett: March 28, 2020

Me: Hi! I hope you are doing okay. This must be immeasurably difficult for you all. I guess I am a bit worried to hear Landon is having friends over. I completely get why you think he needs that. But please consider what is here, out of protection for your broader family.

Brett:: Yes. Very limited. Oklahoma not yet to shelter in place.

Me: That just means your governor has his head up his ass, not that there's no risk. You have more cases there. Kids transmit while asymptomatic and while not harmed themselves they can bring it back to everyone. That's why Roy who lives for his grandkids isn't seeing them at all. And unlike me, he's not scared of much.

Brett: He has preexistings so he has to be careful.

Me: So do you.

Text to Brett: March 29, 2020

Me Looks like Tulsa went to shelter in place yesterday?

Brett: Yes. So we are doing the 6 feet distance. Landon has had almost no contact with anyone but me and April for 2 weeks. Good chance we don't have it unless he has been a symptom free carrier. No way to know.

Eventually, public health experts advised that people could safely see their extended families so long as everyone was outdoors, separated by 6 feet, and masked. So we hosted Roy's daughter and granddaughters for occasional visits in our backyard, and Henry and Brett met up for a visit and takeout dinner in a nearby park.

I told myself I would be praised one day for my extreme caution once we all emerged from the pandemic having never gotten sick with Covid-19. But what seemed prudent behavior at the time later became a source of regret when Brett died having only seen his son twice during 2020.

———— □ ————

I was surprised when Henry told me his dad wondered aloud if he would live to see his next birthday. Brett who called me Apocalyptic Polly always seemed himself unflappably optimistic. It gave me pause and I suddenly realized birthdays — and all holidays — would carry greater significance during the pandemic.

Text to Brett: April 4, 2020

Me: Happy Birthday! 🎂

Brett: Great birthday so far. Landon woke up before me and gave me a hug!

Me: I sure hope it's a good day for you.

Apocalyptic Polly

President Trump said he wanted the country opened back up and returned to normal by Easter on April 12. Public health officials said that was far too soon for public gatherings if the nation was to contain the spread of the virus. The governor of Kansas was sued by churches when she issued an executive order just before Easter, limiting public gatherings to no more than 10 people. Ultimately, life was not back to normal. Most churches were empty Easter Sunday, as socially distanced clergy now led worship services online.

> **Text to Brett:** April 12, 2020
>
> **Me:** If you go to Washington National Cathedral on YouTube, they are doing something cool today. 100 remote singers blended into a choir.
>
> **Me:** BTW, Happy Easter. 🐰
>
> **Brett:** Yes. Happy Easter to you. What a blessing each passing year is.

Though the three of us were living in self-imposed exile, my husband and I managed to visit Denmark, Iceland, Norway, Germany, Great Britain, Ireland, France, and Australia — all from the safety of the living room sofa, as we binged foreign crime dramas on Netflix. No trip, though, was as strange as the one to an exotic animal park in Oklahoma. The Netflix series "Tiger King" became a national guilty pleasure during the pandemic. No matter how strange this new pandemic world was, nothing compared with the bizarre world of Joe Exotic, a gay polygamist and one-time Oklahoma gubernatorial candidate building an empire off public desire to be photographed holding tiger cubs.

"Tiger King" was released early in the pandemic when, according to The New York Post, Americans were watching an average of eight hours of streaming services a day. Notice I didn't say watching television. Increasingly, younger people watched streaming services on their phones and laptops. Henry would spend hours a day lying in bed, staring into his tiny screen. His room was his refuge from his parents while stuck at home with us during lockdown, and his cell phone his way to escape.

I did manage to lure Henry out of his room to sit in front of the television with me on occasion to play video games. Nintendo saw record sales during the pandemic due to demand from people in lockdown looking for something to do. When Nintendo's Wii gaming system came out in 2006 — when Henry was 9 — the units were so hard to come by that Henry and I joked the revolutionary accelerometer technology in the controllers must be made of polar bear teeth.

We didn't manage to get a Wii until after Christmas that year but played Mario Kart regularly until he left for college in 2014. The game system still worked reliably well when we started playing again in 2020, but I suggested perhaps it was time to finally upgrade. Henry said we should get a Nintendo Switch.

First introduced in 2017, the Nintendo Switch retailed for about $300 but by spring of 2020 it was nearly impossible to get at that price. A Switch game called Animal Crossing was taking America by storm. Released March 20, 2020, the family-friendly game, featuring cutesy animals working together in harmony in beautiful settings, was ideal pandemic escapism. The demand for Animal Crossing drove demand for the Switch, causing it to regularly sell out at major retailers. Henry made a sport of hunting it on the secondary market — eBay and other online outlets where game scalpers sold Switch consoles at a markup.

Messenger: April 24, 2020

Me: Have you found us a Switch yet? I need something else in my life besides Crunch Berries in the morning and nightly TV on the couch ... and eavesdropping your physics professors ...

Henry: It looks like the market price is about $492.

Me: Yikes.

Henry: And that's for delivery by May 6.

Me: Too high.

Henry: It's available for $300 at a store in East Lansing, MI. Only a 13.5-hour drive away.

Me: LOL

I relented to the black-market markup and told Henry I was willing to pay half — as a gift for his birthday. We soon had our Switch and established a daily routine of playing Mario games in late afternoon: Mario Kart 8, Mario Odyssey, and Luigi's Mansion 3. Watching Henry vacuum up coins and beat ghosts senseless in Luigi's haunted mansion was remarkably relaxing and satisfying. As good as Xanax. And so much better than facing the real world. ❖

CHAPTER 4

The Revolution Will Be Live-Streamed

When I first heard about the death of George Floyd in Minneapolis, I didn't realize it was new news. Another unarmed Black man killed at the hands of police? There had been so many. Eric Garner, 43, in New York City; Michael Brown, 18, in Ferguson, Missouri; Tamir Rice, 12 in Cleveland, Ohio; all in 2014. Two years before that, 17-year-old Trayvon Martin shot in Florida by a civilian neighborhood watchman. A year after, Freddie Gray, 25, of Baltimore, Maryland, and Sandra Bland, 28, of Texas both died in police custody.

There was nothing new, unfortunately, about unarmed Black people dying at the hands of police. What was new was the increasing number of incidents recorded by bystanders with cell phone cameras. Viral videos of outrageous acts brought world scrutiny; no video did so more than the video recorded by 17-year-old Darnella Frazier and posted to Facebook: It showed former Minneapolis police officer Derek Chauvin kneeling on Floyd's neck. For 9 minutes and 29 seconds. Darnella would later be awarded an honorary Pulitzer.

"Can you believe that video?" my son asked me.

I did not know what he was talking about. I spent my days in the backyard with the cats trying to tune out as much news as possible. My Facebook posts on May 26 were about our bird feeders. I quickly learned what he meant when my Facebook feed filled with the public mourning of my Black women friends. That George Floyd cried out for his mama while dying with a knee upon his neck surfaced profound pain among friends who expressed palpable fear it could be their child next.

Floyd died on Monday, May 25. On Tuesday, Darnella's video went viral, and Minneapolis erupted into protests that continued for days. Police used tear gas and rubber bullets to quell the crowds. Some businesses, including restaurants and an auto-parts store, were set on fire. Unrest grew through the week, spreading to other major cities, including mine. According to the New York Times, by the end of June 2020, more than 4,700 demonstrations had occurred in the United States with an estimated 26 million total participants.

My son wanted to join the local demonstrations in Wichita, which drew 2,000 on May 30. The only reason he didn't was due to my pleading that he not join the crowds and risk bringing Covid-19 and potential death into our home. Just that Monday, the same day Floyd died, the Kansas governor had banned public observances of Memorial Day to reduce community spread. But I understood why the Black families I knew did a different risk-calculus: They feared the virus less than they feared continued injustice and could remain silent no longer.

Still, most protest organizers directed participants to wear masks as a caution against the virus, and most did. Gatherings nationwide were mostly peaceful, but incidents of violence and property damage did occur, and TV newscasts showed footage of burning storefronts in Portland, Oregon, on a loop, leading many critics including President Trump to label the protesters rioters. He threatened to bring the military down upon them.

Millions more clashed online, debates raging in the comments sections of news media. Already badly fractured by differing responses to Covid-19, divisions between family and friends deepened as people raged over whether to say, "Black Lives Matter" or "All Lives Matter." I stood with BLM and even pushed back against those who said setting fires to property was no way to protest. As I listened to the Black voices being elevated that week, for the first time, "no justice, no peace" made sense to me. Why keep the peace of your oppressor? Why respect the authority that has systematically for centuries not respected you?

> **Facebook:** May 31, 2020
>
> *I want to thank my Black teachers. You have taught me the difference between not being racist and being anti-racist. You have taught me why saying "I don't see color" is being blind to what's unique to your experience. You've taught me why the phrase "American melting pot" promotes amalgamation and assimilation, not diversity. You've taught me not to ask you to share your story so I understand, because to do so is to ask you to relive your trauma for my benefit. You have taught me not to ask you to explain Black people as though you are not all different. You've taught me what's good about a white ally and what's not about a white savior. You've taught me that it's helpful to express pain in the face of racism, but unhelpful to make it about my pain and not yours. I see you, I am listening, I will surely keep getting things wrong, but I'm learning, so thank you … to the people who took time to have hard conversations to educate me. You did not owe that to me.* ♥

Though I did not leave the safety of my home, I was intently interested in the protests going on locally. An independent journalist named Meeko gave me a window on events by broadcasting nightly via Facebook livestream. He had a professional video camera setup, the mindset of a documentarian and a fearlessness in the face of occasional gunfire that made his broadcasts riveting. The counter on his live feeds showed more than 80,000 people watching simultaneously during a protest just a few miles from my house. Wichita

Apocalyptic Polly

Eagle photographer Travis Heying was also in the middle of the fray.

> **Facebook:** June 3, 2020
>
> **Travis Heying:** *Wild night in Wichita. Protest at 21st and Maize was peaceful, until some outside forces stirred it up. Police moved in afterwards to flush everyone out. 21st and Arkansas was a whole other story. Looting happening at the QuikTrip. Police moved in with flash grenades. I'd have more pics to share, but that's about the time someone decided they needed one of my cameras more than me. It was a hell of a tug of war for a while, but the risk was quickly becoming greater than the reward. He won.*

Video images of cities ablaze during George Floyd protests blurred together with other scenes of a world afire — an image so pervasive that by Christmas 2020, the year would be symbolized with dumpster fire ornaments.

It began in January with images of scorched koala bears. Though bushfires have been common to Australia for millions of years, the wildfires of 2020 were declared "the worst wildlife disaster in modern history" by the World Wildlife Fund, which estimated three billion animals were destroyed or displaced. Scientists blamed climate changes for producing the dry conditions that led to the extremes. Feeling helpless, I donated money to Australia wildlife rescues.

We were also inundated with images of smoking wreckage from a Boeing 737 Ukrainian civilian airliner with 176 people aboard. The plane crashed on January 8, shortly after takeoff from a Tehran airport, killing all those aboard. Passengers included 138 traveling to Canada via Ukraine, many of whom were Iranian Canadians affiliated with Canadian universities returning from Christmas break.

The college students and others were collateral damage in escalating tensions between the United States and Iran. The tensions had been running so hot between the countries that Henry wondered aloud if he would be drafted into a war with Iran. Five days earlier, the U.S. had authorized a drone strike killing an Iranian general in retaliation for an attack on the U.S. embassy on December 31, 2019, and hours after Iran had launched missiles at U.S. bases in Iraq.

Messenger: January 8, 2020

Me: The Telegraph is reporting that Ukraine is not ruling out the plane being downed by a missile.

Henry: Would we really have shot down an airplane that close to Tehran? Seems unlikely.

Me: I think it's more likely that Iran fucked up and one of their missiles hit a plane with Iranians on it.

Henry: Yes, that seems more likely.

Me: Officials and media seem to be treading on eggshells not to suggest that is what happened, but at the same time every air carrier is suddenly avoiding the air space. No American media is reporting this theory but British media is all over it.

Henry: Iran would have a great incentive to cover this up.

Iranian officials initially disavowed any responsibility for bringing down the airliner blaming mechanical issues at first, but by January 10 Iran publicly admitted the civilian plane had been misidentified as a threat and brought down by two anti-aircraft missiles.

The cumulative effect of constantly hearing about external threats — a global pandemic, possible wars, climate change, widespread job loss, and growing political unrest — put us all on constant alert. The heightened anxiety made us easy targets for those using fear to manipulate.

In the wake of George Floyd, anonymous agitators spread warnings on social media that Black Lives Matter and Antifa activists would be coming to terrorize white neighborhoods in small towns, including in suburban Wichita. The warnings led some towns to impose curfews and board up downtown windows. It also prompted armed citizens to show up en masse, prepared to defend against attacks that never materialized.

I was startled how many people I knew took this as a credible threat. It brought me to the uncomfortable realization that the idea of Black criminality was so pervasive, even those who believe themselves not racist were subject to irrational fear. I shouted into the social media void.

Facebook: June 4, 2020

Me: *There's been a nationwide effort to make you feel afraid of your fellow man — and it's pure insidious manipulation meant to bring division and pain. If you know people in the BLM movement you recognize these fake threats for the absolute crap they are. Your unfounded fear of people who don't look like you is getting black people killed. Stop the fear and save lives. It's that simple.*

K—: *I am duly afraid of mob mentality and rioters. Has nothing to do with race. I avoid protests overseas & I'll avoid them here as they can turn in an instant.*

Me: *Well until your life is threatened in a manner that you feel the need to protest or riot as the better option, you will surely be fine steering clear.*

K—: *My point is that there is a valid reason to fear your fellow man, independent of race. The Antifa posts were scary. Antifa is scary due to their tactics.*

Me: *The posts weren't actually from Antifa apparently. Time will tell for sure. Not that I am defending Antifa. I can't tell if they are real or a straw man.*

K—: *I did not believe the Antifa posts were real, but they scared me, nonetheless. I tried to find if there was an actual Twitter account by that name & did not see one, so I questioned its validity. Yes, the ugliest part of all of this is the manipulation of information.*

Looking back, it's hard to know why the death of George Floyd — occurring in the middle of a pandemic — had such a dramatic effect, but it did. Within days, cultural norms shifted in support of Black America. Not enough to correct hundreds of years of injustice and the resulting disparity in generational wealth, but it signaled substantive change might finally be possible.

Corporate America — sensing the shift — responded with public statements condemning police killings of unarmed Black people and supporting peaceful protest, while also announcing hundreds of millions of dollars investment in efforts to address racial inequality. Notably, the NFL reversed its policy of requiring players to stand or remain in the locker room during the national anthem, a position originally taken after player Colin Kaepernick in 2016 took a knee during the anthem in a silent protest of racism and police brutality in America. NASCAR, the sanctioning body of stock car racing popular in the South, announced it would ban the Confederate flag from appearing at its races.

Within a month, Southern cities and some independent activists began removing Confederate war statues that had stood for a hundred years. Critics accused BLM vandals of attempting to erase American history, but in fact most statues were removed by government officials acting on behalf of public will. The biggest shocker was when the state of Mississippi — as approved by its Legislature and governor — elected to remove the Confederate cross symbol from its own state flag. The rapid shift toward racial justice offered a glimmer of hope in a bleak year. ❖

CHAPTER 5

Worn on the Fourth of July

I spontaneously entered the Mask Wars on the 3rd of July, the day our Wichita City Council by a single vote opted to require people to wear masks.

Advocates for the ordinance had been pushing for months. Acting on public health advice that mask-wearing significantly reduces community spread of Covid-19, the Kansas governor implemented a mask requirement by executive order. The Legislature came into special session to curtail the governor's powers and put mask ordinance decisions in local government hands. Our County Commission kept voting against requiring masks, but then the City Council reversed again.

Giddy over the public health victory, I impulsively decided to start a Facebook group to support mask wearing. I called it Mask Up ICT. Like many well-intended efforts, it was a disaster. The group attracted 500 members in the first 24 hours, 1,000 members in the first 48. There were 2,400 members by 72 hours, when I gave up.

Facebook: July 3, 2020

On July 3, 2020, the City of Wichita adopted an ordinance requiring the use of masks in public areas. This was at the request of local public health experts who believe masks will slow the spread of Covid-19 and save lives in our community. The ordinance provides a "stick" — fines for failure to comply. We want to provide the carrot — the promise of financial support by consumers who appreciate mask usage. Please submit your recommendations for businesses, nonprofits, and restaurants to be listed here

Facebook: July 6, 2020

Hello all! I am archiving this group. It's simply too overwhelming for me to keep up with. I never imagined it would grow so big so fast. I think people want something different and I encourage someone to create it. I need to resume my life. Be safe and well.

What happened during the time between those two posts was an ugly lesson in social media tribal dynamics. I had created the group with the purpose of providing accurate information that supported people who were complying with the ordinance. At first, most posters cooperated — probably because most original members came from my personal friends' group. People cheerfully posted selfies of their masked faces and traded tips on where to find patterns and buy colorful fabrics for homemade masks.

But soon I was dealing with an increasing number of strangers who insisted on using the group to publicly shame businesses that were not complying with the ordinance. I tried to maintain control, deleting all negative posts. When that wasn't enough, I set the controls so that I had to approve each post. I did not approve the negative ones and told people why: I did not want my Facebook group to become a forum for unsubstantiated rumors and angry criticisms that harmed local businesspeople.

I begged people to keep it positive. An increasing number insisted on being negative. They took their negativity to the comments on existing posts, which were much harder for me to police than new posts. "Why are you deleting our comments?" they demanded. I suggested to a few individuals they start their own group if they wanted a place to out the bad actors.

I was incredulous at how quickly members of a group I created not 48 hours earlier felt entitled to set their own rules. I was attacked for not being one of them, not fully in the fight if I wasn't going to allow posts that criticized places not requiring masks.

The irony of this was it was all immaterial to me personally. My household of three rarely wore masks because we went nowhere but the occasional doctor's appointment.

I spent July 4th weekend glued to my cell phone, constantly approving new members and policing comments. I couldn't sleep; when I did, the poison spread. Finally, in the early hours of the morning of July 6, I archived the group, allowing it to remain online but no new comments or posts to be added. A few people begged me to put it back up, offering to help me moderate the group. I said no, I felt it was a lost cause, a snake pit of vitriol I no longer wanted to be a part of.

And those were the people I agreed with. Fact was, they were not much better than the crackpots who said masks were a government conspiracy to subjugate the masses, not unlike the stars worn by Jews during the Holocaust.

Facebook: July 26, 2020

Reading Facebook comments in the middle of the night is a bad idea. It's full of monsters in the closet and under the bed. The idea that there are such deranged, hate-filled people believing nonsense is nightmarish. Are these people real? Are they trouble-making trolls? Are they mentally ill? Are they armed? Sheesh. I want to know nothing of such people. 👹💀☠️

CHAPTER **6**

Fall Will Make It Better

Even as public health officials warned that fall would bring a second wave of virus, it was hard not to feel optimism as the season changed. A viral video by the comedic Holderness Family captured my mood as the wife maniacally retrieves fall decorations from her attic and begins adorning every corner of her house with pumpkins, cornucopia, and cornstalks, repeating as though in a trance, "Fall will fix it! Fall with fix it!"

Beauty was fading in the backyard that had served as my refuge from the pandemic and the claustrophobia. Sunflowers, the last flowers to bloom, wilted over. Green increasingly gave way to brown. Bees and butterflies no longer stopped by. Still in self-imposed exile, I wondered how I could get the pumpkins and mums necessary to transform the landscape. Neither DoorDash nor Instacart nor Amazon could bring me pumpkins. It was too strange a request to put upon a friend, I thought.

I couldn't do anything about the pandemic, the upcoming presidential election, the wildfires now burning across the American West, or people separated from families and friends, or patients dying alone in overburdened hospitals. Decorating for fall could provide a small measure of joy, at least.

Walmart provided the answer. A new service called Walmart+ would deliver anything from the store, no delivery fee during the initial trial. I ordered 20 pumpkins in different sizes, three baskets of mums, and a decorative scarecrow for good measure. I used these to decorate not only the front porch, but also the view from my chair under the tree in the backyard. Never had I so needed something pretty to look at.

A good view only gets you so far. Six months into the pandemic, we were feeling increasingly anxious. My husband developed a habit of waking at 4 a.m. My son's OCD symptoms worsened. I developed something called "health anxiety," compulsively Googling the myriad odd aches, pains, and other physical symptoms I was experiencing to see if I had Covid-19 or something else.

A Harvard medical study found 2 out of 3 Americans had more difficulty sleeping during the pandemic, and 1 out of 3 worried "a lot" or "extremely" about societal breakdown. Everyone looked for a way to cope, and many — particularly women — found it in drinking more. Alcohol sales spiked during the initial shutdowns. That wasn't an option in my house as Roy is a recovering alcoholic, so we never bring alcohol in the house.

Ready to try anything, I noticed a friend commenting on social media about her daughter finding so much relief from a weighted blanket she bought one for herself. Originally introduced to help children with autism, they became more widely popular as people struggled with sleep. There is no conclusive scientific evidence around the benefits of weighted blankets, but the theory is they provide deep pressure stimulation, stimulating the production of mood-boosting serotonin, reducing the stress hormone cortisol, and increasing melatonin, a hormone that helps you sleep.

According to *sleepfoundation.org*: "By distributing an even amount of weight and pressure across the body, weighted blankets may calm the fight-or-flight response and activate the relaxing parasympathetic nervous system in preparation for sleep."

I bought myself one online — a 15 lb. blanket wrapped in a fuzzy duvet — and immediately found I felt calmer, like a swaddled baby, but noticed a side effect of extra vivid dreams. Roy said he wanted one, too, so I ordered him one, then one for Henry. We all three had our blankets by September 18, 2020, when Supreme Court Justice Ruth Bader Ginsberg died, and President Trump immediately promised to push through a replacement before the end of his term. My husband and I were agitated; my son was despondent.

Messenger: September 18, 2020, 12:12 a.m.
Henry: I was trying to get to sleep but I haven't been able to.

Me: Get under that weighted blanket.

Roy and I had extra money for things like pumpkins and weighted blankets thanks to our adjunct gig teaching a fall class at the university where I worked and Henry attended graduate school. At both the university level and at the local public schools, students and instructors were given a choice to either attend classes in person or remotely. Our family opted for remote. I had spent most of August trying to learn the technical skills necessary to teach a class by Zoom. Our class normally met for three hours, but because no one wants to sit in front of a screen for three hours — unless binging Netflix! — we cut it to an hour and a half.

Students would no longer engage in discussions or journal during class time but "asynchronously" — a new pandemic buzzword — on their own time. I learned how to create and share PowerPoints through Zoom, how to record Zoom lectures and upload them to YouTube for students' later viewing, and how to use Blackboard — the university's platform for online learning — to manage and grade student discussions and journals.

Instead of sitting next to each other as we would in a classroom, Roy and I sat in different rooms in our homes where we could each get a strong Wi-Fi signal and where the sound of our voices wouldn't create feedback. We took pictures of the bookcases in our homes and used them for Zoom backgrounds so it appeared we were in the same room. Eavesdropping on Henry's classes I realized not every instructor was learning these new skills. Some set up laptop cameras in their classrooms aimed at them teaching at the white board as they always had.

But the hardest part of teaching online wasn't technical. It was staring into the void of black boxes on a screen rather than student faces. There was one student who consistently kept her camera on during class. I would configure my screen to see her so I could watch her face and have some idea if I was connecting.

The strain of all this change and social isolation took an obvious toll on our students, and on my son. Henry thought he was the only one struggling to stay motivated to do schoolwork and meet deadlines. I assured him he was not. Our students were suffering the most incredible distractions: One student was frequently absent because she was an ER nurse's aide, frequently called in to work extra shifts. Others got sick with Covid-19 or had family members fall ill. All of them complained of mental health challenges brought on by the loneliness, the fear, and the political upheaval; depression and anxiety plagued us all. A study by the CDC had reported in June 2020 that 1 in 4 young adults between the ages of 18-24 had thoughts of suicide in the preceding 30 days.

Text to Brett: August 4, 2020

Me: Henry had a rough day yesterday. It was tough. He had several frustrations getting his new computer to work. He is better today. But it's not just about the computer. It's about self-doubt about the semester. He's so afraid of failing. I told him these are the most challenging times I have ever lived through and if he wants to just sit out the semester that is a valid choice. I'm not sure he took the idea seriously. But I do think it's a valid option. Maybe necessary for all our mental health. What do you think?

Brett: I will talk to him.

Brett: Yes. Strange times.

On September 9, news broke that President Trump — who had spent the year dismissing the Covid-19 threat, undercutting public health experts, and scoring political points with followers who labeled it a hoax — had been recorded on tape by Watergate journalist Bob Woodward admitting he wasn't straight with Americans. "This is deadly stuff," Trump told Woodward on February 7. Woodward did not reveal Trump's comments until the release of his book, "Rage," seven months later.

CNN.com, September 9, 2020

*Trump says the job of a president is "to keep our country safe."
But in early February, Trump told Woodward he knew how
deadly the virus was, and in March, admitted he kept that
knowledge hidden from the public.*

*"I wanted to always play it down," Trump told Woodward
on March 19, even as he had declared a national emergency
over the virus days earlier. "I still like playing it down, because
I don't want to create a panic."*

If instead of playing down what he knew, Trump had acted decisively in early February with a strict shutdown and a consistent message to wear masks, social distance and wash hands, experts believe that thousands of American lives could have been saved.

How you reacted to this revelation depended a lot on how you reacted to Trump. Fox News Radio host Jimmy Failla said, "A sane person might recognize the value of promoting societal calm in the face of a once-in-a-century global pandemic." Others attacked journalist Woodward for holding back Trump's admission for his book release. Ultimately, the revelation seemed to have no impact. A significant part of the population continued to believe Covid-19 was a hoax, while the rest of us lived in fear.

Facebook: September 9, 2020

Me: *Projecting optimism is fine for a parent trying to protect children from adult issues. It's an effective strategy for boosting stock prices or cajoling (conning?) investors. But it's a rotten idea in a situation that requires leading people to willingly change their behavior to confront a public health threat. By denying the truth, all he has done is sow doubt and distrust of the people trying to solve the problem and save lives.*

S——: *Idk, Polly. Just think how much better things would things have turned out if we had a guy like this when Pearl Harbor was attacked?* 😐 😕

My cats were no longer a source of solace. When I started spending more time with them in the spring, I soon noticed Mr. Boots wasn't well. A neighbor remarked on him looking thin. She was right. I soon noticed he wasn't eating as much. Watching him, I thought it was a dental problem, so I switched him from dry food to wet. I waited longer than I should have to take him to the vet, leaning into agoraphobia as I was.

By July it became clear I had to do something. On more than one occasion, he appeared dead, taking long to rouse when I jostled him. I was pleased to discover a local vet doing curbside check in. I would simply bring Mr. Boots in a cat carrier, wait in the car for a vet tech to retrieve him, consult with the doctor by phone, then give my credit card to pay over the phone.

The diagnosis was not good. Mr. Boots had heartworms. In dogs, the disease is treatable. In cats, it can only be prevented, not cured. I had not prevented it because I had no idea of the threat. Cats get heartworm disease from mosquitoes. The worms transferred to their bloodstream lodge and grow in their hearts. Toxins released caused acute respiratory symptoms, periodic vomiting, weight loss, and death.

My initial reaction was shame that in trying to protect my family from disease I had endangered my cat's life. Of course, it's not so simple. My real error was ignorance about his need for monthly heartworm medication once he became an outdoor cat. These were not concerns of strictly indoor cats.

There was no cure, only palliative treatment to extend his life, the vet said. She prescribed a steroid that I would need to give him once a day. Thus began an elaborate routine of bringing Mr. Boots indoors to eat separately from Noel, to ensure he got the meds I put in his food. We kept him in an enclosed pop-up tent by the TV. For months, he did remarkably well on steroids. (Perhaps that's why the term "on steroids" means what it does.) It was a relief.

Facebook: September 24, 2020

How is anyone supposed to concentrate on anything routine and mundane with everything going on in the world that one friend, who is not given to hyperbole, described as apocalyptic?

Apocalyptic Polly

Somehow, we did establish routines. Mine began in the morning, waking up, drinking coffee, eating Crunch Berries, feeding the cat, loading the dishwasher, taking meds to keep depression and anxiety at bay, and heading downstairs to work in my basement office. Roy would work at the dining table, writing a family history. Henry would join me downstairs about midmorning to attend his classes remotely and surf online, and unload dishes as needed.

Henry frequently updated me on news of the day and the latest presidential polling numbers being reported by 528, a website maintained by a journalist statistician named Nate Silver. Nate predicted Trump would lose and the Democrats would regain Congress. The odds on that changed daily and Henry kept me updated on that while Roy updated his Facebook daily with the total number dead from Covid. By October, deaths numbered in the 200,000s.

Everyone was on their own for lunch. Henry and I ate together downstairs because Roy objected to us sitting at his work desk, the dining table. Around 3:30 or 4 p.m. I would break away from work and call Henry to come play video games. By 5 p.m., I would start on dinner and tell Roy to clear the table. Serving dinner for my family became a ritual of rebellion against the disorder imposed on our lives. I made a home-cooked meal five nights a week. On Wednesdays and Saturdays, we ordered DoorDash.

Once we all sat down to dinner, I would say, *"Alexa, play NPR News"* and get a five-minute summary of the day's events, and always, the latest death toll from Covid-19. I wondered if this is what it felt like for my mom, growing up listening to the daily news about World War II on the radio. Both of us trying to maintain routines while living through difficult times, day after day, wondering when it would end.

After dinner, Roy would clear and rinse the dishes, I would give Mr. Boots his medicine, and then Roy and I would meet up on the living room couch for an evening of escapism watching European crime dramas. Henry would retreat to his room to listen to podcasts and surf news reports. And the next day, we would do it all over again. It became very hard to tell the days apart or remember what day it was, even what month. When the seasons changed, I marked the occasion by changing the wreath on the front door.

—————— ▭ ——————

Approaching holidays brought a respite from the sameness, but also a new thing for the nation to argue over: how to celebrate Halloween. Hershey's, the chocolate manufacturer, launched a website featuring ideas for celebrating Halloween safely during a pandemic. It included a map featuring the Covid-19 risk level in each county, to be used as a guide for choosing activities based on community risk level. Low community risk? Go ahead with traditional trick-or-treating or costume parties, preferably outdoors and socially distanced. High risk? Suggestions included Zoom parties or reverse trick-or-treating where kids stay in their own yards and adults drive by, handing candy out through car windows.

Such ideas were intended to be helpful, but parents complained their kids were yet again being cheated of childhood joy because of the pandemic. Many railed against public health officials who discouraged traditional trick-or-treating, fearing it becoming a super-spreader event. Some inventive folks developed treat chutes to drop candy into children's buckets from 6 feet distance. Others opposed Halloween altogether, arguing children bunching up on porch stoops was dangerous; they suggested decorating houses but not handing out candy. We opted to leave our porch light off and stayed in watching horror movies, playing Luigi Mansion 3, and binging on homemade jack-o'-lantern cookies.

It was all a temporary distraction. The thing that scared us most was still three days away — Election Day. ❖

CHAPTER **7**

It's the End
of the Election,
and I Feel Fine

Heading into Election Day on Nov. 3, 2020, Henry assured me that Nate Silver's 528 website predicted Joe Biden had an 89% chance of winning the election, Democrats had a 97% chance of keeping the majority in House and 75% chance of flipping the Senate.

Ultimately, Biden would win with 51% of the popular vote to Trump's 47%, enough to secure 303 electoral votes to Trump's 232. Democrats maintained majority in the House, despite losing 10 seats. The Senate split 50-50, with Democrats technically winning control given Vice President Kamala Harris would now hold the deciding vote.

But we didn't know any of that when we went to bed on Election Day. Instead the nation began a period of disorienting uncertainty that lasted months. The presidential election was called for Biden on Nov. 7, but Trump refused to concede, making unsubstantiated allegations embraced by his followers that the election was rigged. He chiefly blamed states that liberalized absentee and vote-by-mail balloting to reduce community spread of the virus. It is not exaggeration to say that for a while we appeared headed for constitutional crisis or possibly civil war.

Facebook: November 3, 2020

So here's the deal:

I am safe and healthy. I have the privilege of working from home and ability to have meals and groceries delivered. And yet ... I am desperately worried about the impact of Covid-19 on my community because our ICU beds are full and nurses maxed and that means people I don't even know may die, and I want to do whatever I can to prevent that.

I am financially secure, and my retirement fund is doing great along with the stock market. And yet ... I am desperately worried about the people unemployed and underemployed because of the pandemic and because of a system that makes people like me wealthier while the half of America not invested in the stock market works harder for less money every year, and I want to do everything I can to change that.

I am white, and straight, and I am a citizen, all by chance of birth. I have privilege. I do not worry about what might happen if police pull me over. I do not worry about my spouse or parents being deported. I do not worry about whether a Supreme Court ruling might capriciously annul my marriage. And yet ... I want to do everything I can to alleviate the suffering of my friends impacted by social injustice.

This is why the outcome of this election literally feels like life or death to me, even though I will probably be okay either way. Because it is not about me, and I cannot feel safe when others are not.

Fears of societal collapse aside, I was about to feel a whole other level of unsafe. A week after the election, my stepdaughter, her husband, and their three daughters were all positive for Covid-19.

Apocalyptic Polly

Rose had done everything in her power to keep her family safe from the virus. She and the girls went almost nowhere. They opted for remote schooling, kept friends and the extended family including my husband out of the house, used curbside grocery pickup. It was isolating and painful and particularly burdensome to a family with special needs children. But Marc, her husband, still had to go to work to support this family of five. Not everyone at his workplace observed the same precautions. Marc got sick first, then Rose, their teen daughter O—, and the 8-year-old twin girls, N— and C—. They all had fevers and other symptoms.

Just days before the diagnosis, Rose shared a Facebook memory from the same date three years before, showing daughter N—- sick in the E.R., using the post to explain why they would not be attending large family gatherings at Thanksgiving — the latest subject of heated division:

Facebook: November 5, 2020

Rose: *Just in case anyone thinks we are overreacting to coronavirus, this is exactly how sick C—and N— get with normal seasonal viruses, and several times a year normally, although usually I can keep their temps from going over 105. (When we last rushed C—to the hospital, she had spiked a temp to 107 and had gone gray.) It comes with constant vomiting and I normally have to feed them liquids from medicine droppers, alternate meds and not sleep because I'm setting alarms each hour. They miss WEEKS of school at a time, sometimes with fevers lasting 10 days or longer. If you think this is a partisan issue, I have an issue with your logic. ***We will not be attending events including holidays, we will not be helping people move, we will not be available to chat in person.*** Please don't drop by the house wanting to speak to us, we are available by phone. If anyone has an issue with us over this, look at that picture of N—again and ask if you would really rather risk her life AND C—'s than take this seriously.*

I worried and Roy raged.

Facebook: November 19, 2020

Roy: *My daughter Rose Rachel is on her 13th straight day of fever, infected with Covid-19; her husband Marc has it, as do her twins N— and C—, as does O—, her 15-year-old. Rose is still at home, in bed, but her oxygen level has dropped to 94% at times, just a hair away from what would prompt an ER trip and hospitalization. Her twins have vulnerabilities that could cause great harm if their infections escalate. All hospitals in Wichita are beyond full, their staffs worn out from overwork. Topeka hospitals are now ventilating people in hallways. Most of this public crisis could be avoided if we didn't live next to geniuses like some of you who claim, against common sense, that the crisis is fake, and political, and that you're taking a stand against tyrannical government bent on "dictating" what you wear on your face. You have lost all common decency. You are not good citizens. You are not Christians — those of you "Christian" posers who say these things. You have done harm; you have killed and sickened many grannies and disabled people who got infected because of your egos, your self-absorbed preaching, your low IQs, and your nose-picking, butt-scratching, yahoo, goat-roper, voodoo, "let's burn the witches" lynch mob beliefs.*

Roy's post drew 147 likes, 53 comments, and was shared 37 times. One comment stood out:

Rose: *But, Dad, how do you really feel? Love you*

When I wrote Henry's Dad, Brett, to tell him about Rose, his reply was prescient.

Text to Brett: December 3, 2020

Me: Don't know if you heard but Rose's family has been sick for 25 days now. Nothing requiring hospitalization though O— went to the ER this morning. X-ray showed her lungs okay. Got an inhaler.

Brett: Covid?

Apocalyptic Polly

Me: Yes

Brett: Landon will complete a full semester at school. Crossing fingers that his school is able to safely complete the semester. After next week he has one week of distance learning.

Brett: Denise (his sister, a public-school educator) has not had a confirmed case of Covid-19. She has been working remotely.

Me I am really disturbed by what is happening with hospitals in OK and KS. Many friends are healthcare workers and they are just slammed.

Brett: Yes. Let's hope we can get through the next few months.

CHAPTER **8**

Only 100 Days 'Til the Christmas Tree Comes Down

Trying to maintain a semblance of tradition at Thanksgiving was a challenge. Our household and extended families followed public health recommendations to celebrate only with our own households. Some inventive families managed to share meals by each preparing different traditional dishes then doing porch drop-offs at each other's houses. I ordered our meal delivered from Cracker Barrel.

Unable to go to his father's house for Thanksgiving as he had the previous year, Henry met up with Brett in a nearby park earlier in November. They shared a takeout steak dinner from Outback, sitting 6 feet apart, then walked and talked for over an hour. It was the second of just two times they saw each other in 2020 — and the last time outside a hospital. When Brett brought Henry back to our house, they stood talking another 20 minutes in the front yard before Brett left. From inside I could hear Brett's booming voice, but agoraphobia kept me from going out to greet him. Another regrettably missed opportunity.

I so badly wanted a traditional Thanksgiving. I brought out special dishes, set a table with chocolate turkeys at each plate, and tried once again to use food as an anchor to normalcy. But nothing was normal. Henry couldn't see his dad or his grandma. Roy couldn't see Rose, who still had Covid-19, or his granddaughters.

And when I turned on the Macy's Parade in the morning — an attempt to relive a Thanksgiving tradition I had shared with my parents as a child — I found a broadcast of empty New York City streets augmented by a virtual-reality rendering of balloons from prior years passing by skyscrapers. The only thing live was a scaled-down show in Herald Square.

Nearly every year of my childhood I had watched the Macy's Parade and the high-kicking Rockettes on TV with my father. Twice Brett and I had attended the parade in person, one time with my mom. A third time, I had taken Henry as a boy. This absence of a parade was unmooring, and made worse because neither Henry nor Roy wanted to watch with me. On Facebook, I posted an image of a cartoon turkey wearing a surgical mask and a Pilgrim's hat, and this:

Facebook: November 26, 2020

Thinking today of everyone missing someone today. We are all urged to be thankful — and there is much to be thankful for — but it's okay to acknowledge sadness and grief that can coexist with appreciation for all we still have. I would hug you if I could.

The day after Thanksgiving I threw myself into another tradition — putting up the Christmas tree. Many friends had already put trees up in early November, a trend that became common as we all yearned to brighten and bring change to our living spaces. I put our tree in the front window, as usual, and covered it with white lights and ornaments dating from my childhood and Henry's, as well as more recent ones collected during travels with Roy. I spent a lot of sleepless nights sitting staring into the glow of that tree during the next 100 days.

———————— ▭ ————————

The first two weeks of December brought relative calm. No major news events. Our lives at home were focused on the windup of the semester — Henry finishing out his coursework and Roy and I grading our students' final papers.

All was not right with the world, by any means. The two weeks following Thanksgiving saw a spike in Covid-19 cases, likely due to the number of people who traveled and gathered with family anyway. I started noticing not just people reporting they were sick, but dear friends whose parents in their 80s and 90s were dying.

But in our immediate world, things seemed calm — so much so that I finally found the strength to address what I had been putting off — health care for myself and my cat, Mr. Boots. My family physician of 20 years retired in September, leaving me without a doctor. Anxiety over everything seemed to manifest as multiple health problems for me. A racing heart, stomachaches, weird recurrent aches and pains in my face and neck, insomnia, and the realization that I hadn't had a period in several weeks. I decided to make an appointment with the doctor who took over my old doctor's practice. The doctor zeroed in on the thing I had been worried the least about: He said my absence of periods could be endometrial cancer. He wanted to run a series of tests.

I came home from the doctor and braced myself for two unpleasant conversations — first to tell my husband, who had lost his father to lung cancer, and whose daughter had what had been termed long-Covid. Roy was matter of fact, his way of coping. He had much on his mind. Rose had just posted about her saga:

Facebook: December 17, 2020

Rose: *Today is day 40 of covid. I still have a fever. Am I a long-hauler? Looks to be the case. O—— still has symptoms that are just a few steps behind mine. She's only 15 but she has struggled with elevated temp, shortness of breath and exhaustion for 37 days. I feel like what I say is futile, that my story is seen as politicized, that it just doesn't matter. I just burst into tears as I, yet again, had to call C—— and N—— into school because I can't get out of bed without my heart feeling like it will explode and my fever spiking. But, I keep posting because, maybe, it'll reach someone. Stay safe. Please take precautions.*

Second, I had to tell my son Henry. I felt like I was outside my body, sitting there next to him, telling him I faced something that might kill me. He surprised me with his calm response. "Mom, there are layers and layers of modern medicine standing between you and death."

The next day I took Mr. Boots to the vet. He was getting worse. The steroids were no longer enough. He was eating less and digestive problems were making for increasingly arduous cleanup. I was not prepared when the vet told me it was time to start thinking about euthanasia. I told her that Mr. Boots still had good days, and I wanted to wait until after Christmas. She said when he had more bad days than good, it was time. Now I had more bad news to share with Henry. He was sad. Mr. Boots had been with us since 2007 when Henry was in middle school.

Those two bits of news and two cancer screens scheduled a week before Christmas overwhelmed me. I tried breathing exercises to deal with increasingly frequent panic attacks. I become obsessed with the idea myself or someone I love was about to die. I had increased body aches and feared going to sleep, believing I might stop breathing.

When I did sleep, I would later wake up during the night shaking. I would get up and stare into the Christmas tree. It didn't help that on December 19, a swarm of earthquakes shook our house.

Facebook: December 19, 2020
Just how much shit are breathing exercises supposed to get us through?

While I worried about death, Henry's more immediate concern seemed to be that he now had a girlfriend, Alexis, whom he met through the dating app Bumble, and I was insisting that any dates they had be outside, with masks on, and 6 feet of social distance between them. Henry was feeling increasingly trapped as a 23-year-old living with his mom and stepdad. He was in no way alone in this. During the pandemic, for the first time since the Great Depression of the 1930s, a majority of 18- to 29-year-olds were living with their parents. His girlfriend, also 23, shared an apartment with her mother.

Determined to do something approximating a normal date, Henry set up a projector in the backyard aimed at the side of the garage. He connected the projector to Wi-Fi, an Amazon Fire streaming stick, and the Switch. Sitting 6 feet apart in folding chairs, while wearing heavy coats and wrapped in blankets, Henry and Alexis sat outside in temperatures in the 30s, watching movies and playing video games. I stayed inside worrying they would freeze to death or die from a tree branch falling off the giant oak above them. (Months later, large limbs did fall onto the exact spot where they had been sitting.)

I went into Christmas wondering if it would be my last. It would most certainly be Mr. Boots' last. I wanted to leave something of us behind, so I threw myself into a project. In 2004, I had published a children's book I wrote called "Santa's Stray." It was inspired by a real stray I named Simon that came into my life immediately after my father had died in 2001. Using the new skills I had learned in teaching our class online, I took photos of each page and using Zoom recorded a video of me showing the pictures while reading the story. I wore a Santa hat and held Mr. Boots in my lap as I read.

I uploaded it on December 21, the solstice, and the same day Jupiter and Saturn were supposed to converge in the sky low on the horizon. Some said the celestial event was a repeat of the Bethlehem Star, which Christians long believed had proclaimed the birth of Christ. No matter if it was true; in a year of darkness it was a light that inspired hope. Henry and his girlfriend planned another socially distanced date to see it, going to the top of a university parking garage after dusk. I walked into the street in front of our house to catch a glimpse. I thought I saw it but wasn't sure.

I did everything in my power to make Christmas joyous for our family, decorating the entire house so it sparkled, playing holiday music and videos, cooking traditional foods, baking traditional cookies, wrapping lots of gifts, mailing out cards with hand-written notes. The weather cooperated.

> **Facebook:** December 24, 2020
> *For the year we've had, it's pretty nice to get both a Bethlehem star and snow for Christmas. Wishing everyone peaceful, tranquil moments.*

Roy noticed my efforts and thanked me. Henry simply expected it. When my sister's husband died on Christmas Eve four years previous, my son had remarked when I briefly considered not baking cookies or doing Christmas as usual, "Mom, I cannot imagine any circumstance in which you did not do Christmas." Henry was right: as long as I live and breathe, I would make a big deal out of Christmas.

But there was no escaping the sadness of separation. Henry missed seeing his dad and his grandma. Roy had not seen his own mother since January and missed seeing his children and grandchildren. Video calls allowed us to close some of the distance, but it was not the same. I cut out of an extended family Zoom gathering early because it brought on a panic attack that was overwhelming.

As December drew to a close, we counted down the days to the end of the pandemic year, as though the year changing would break a horrible spell. We had reason to hope: On December 11, 2020, the Food and Drug Administration granted an emergency use authorization for the Pfizer Covid-19 vaccine. A second vaccine by Moderna received its authorization a week later. We were told the vaccines were more than 90% effective at preventing illness and nearly 100% effective at preventing hospitalization and death.

Health care workers immediately began receiving their first doses. Vaccination would mean families reunited and life returned to normal. We could not wait. And if Democrats retook the White House and Congress? An added bonus — for half of us, anyway. What we couldn't know at the time is many of the same folks who didn't want Biden for president wouldn't want the vaccine either.

Facebook: December 31, 2020

My New Year's Eve wish for you — peace as this year fades into history. May it become a thing that happened that we survived, recognizing of course that some did not. But as we greet tomorrow, may we begin anew and find hope.

CHAPTER 9

This Is Not
My Beautiful New Year

I awoke on January 1, 2021, to 4 inches of beautiful snow. Everything was blanketed in white and silence, but I did not feel peace. The entire nation, it felt, had waited out 2020 as an endurance test. Now the year was over, but little else was.

Covid-19 cases were peaking, and with them the number of daily deaths. Roy's daughter, Rose, continued to suffer daily fevers and exhaustion. Political rancor was as bad as ever, as President Trump still would not accept the outcome of the election. At home, I awaited the results on my biopsy to see if I had endometrial cancer and accepted that New Year's Day would be my last day with my sick cat.

> **Text message to Brett:** January 1, 2021
> **Me:** We're taking Boots to the vet to say goodbye tomorrow. It is definitely time. Henry is pretty upset. He wants to go with me for the euthanasia. He's never done that before but he wants to be there. Wanted you to know.

On the morning of January 2, I made the call to the vet. We were ready to say goodbye. The vet typically made pet owners wait in their cars during the pandemic. They made exceptions for euthanasia. Henry decided he wanted to be there. The three of us went together, me holding Mr. Boots in my lap in the car. He had been increasingly lethargic through the holidays, eating little, his eyes and nose clogged with mucus. But on this final drive, he lifted his head excitedly and looked around at the world passing by. He seemed, for a few moments, genuinely happy.

Once there, a vet tech took Mr. Boots first to prepare him, giving him a sedative, then escorted me and Henry in. This was not my first time to watch someone I love die. There had been other cats, other people. That made it no easier. Every death conjured every previous one in my mind. Henry and I cried during our moments alone with Mr. Boots before the vet came in. Then with our hands on him, us telling him how much we had loved him for the past 13 years, the cat was still as the vet injected the solution. Mr. Boots' head instantly dropped. Lifeless. The vet checked his heart rate. He was gone. Just. Like. That.

Our household was quickly preoccupied with politics. On January 3, Nancy Pelosi was narrowly re-elected speaker of the House. The control of the Senate would be determined on January 5 with the outcome of the Georgia special election runoff, which would decide the fate of both Georgia Senate seats. Democrats won both seats by less than a percentage point, creating a 50-50 split in the Senate. The election of Kamala Harris as vice president — who serves as the deciding vote in the Senate in event of a tie — gave Democrats Senate control.

The presidential race was also tight in Georgia — so much so that Joe Biden won the state's 16 electoral votes by just 11,779 ballots. It was not enough to swing the outcome of the presidential election, but also on January 3, The Washington Post released a recording of a December 23 phone call in which President Trump had pressured the Georgia secretary of state, fellow Republican Brad Raffensperger, to "find" enough votes to give him Georgia's 16 electoral votes. That was not enough votes to change the outcome of the election, but Trump wanted them anyway.

Transcript, December 23, 2020, Phone Call Recording

> **Trump:** *"The people of Georgia are angry, the people of the country are angry. ... And there's nothing wrong with saying, you know, that you've recalculated."*

> **Raffensperger:** *"Well, Mr. President, the challenge that you have is, the data you have is wrong."*

Like every other time Trump was caught on tape doing or saying something suspect, it had no consequential effect on his supporters. Trump's efforts to overturn the election heated up on January 5 when he publicly called on Vice President Mike Pence to reject the results of the Electoral College when they come before Congress on January 6. "The Vice President has the power to reject fraudulently chosen electors," Trump tweeted.

All of this made the coming events of January 6 — and by that I mean simply the official tallying of the Electoral College ballots — an event akin to the Super Bowl at our house. Which is how Roy, Henry, and I came to be watching the live feed of ballot counting at the moment there was commotion on the Senate floor as Pence was suddenly removed from the chamber by the Secret Service. Curious as to what was happening, we switched over to news channels and could not believe what we saw: Live news coverage of a swarm of hundreds of Trump supporters climbing over barricades, up walls, and through windows. They had come to Washington at Trump's urging, to participate in the "Stop the Steal" demonstration. Now they were storming the U.S. Capitol, supposedly, we were being told by newscasters, to stop the counting of the ballots. To stop Biden from being elected.

Sitting on the sofa watching the events unfold with my husband and son, my first impulse was to text Brett, Henry's father. I could not think of Washington and the Capitol without thinking of Brett. Nor could I think of governmental overthrow.

We met in 1985, my freshman year of college, in a seminar class that overlapped my interests with his: "U.S.-Soviet Relations as Reflected in the Print Media." He was finishing a bachelor's degree in philosophy; I was starting a degree in journalism. We both studied Russian language and literature. By 1991 we were married two years, and I had just completed my master's degree when we went to Moscow to work for an English-language paper — me as a reporter and him as an interpreter. When I left early from the strain, he stayed a few weeks more and witnessed the collapse of the Soviet Union, August 19-21, 1991 — three days where he walked along lines of armored vehicles listening to political speeches and watching the Russian people resist the communist hardliners.

Later, we lived in D.C., where I worked as a reporter and the U.S. Capitol served as backdrop to our unfolding lives. We lived in a high-rise apartment in Alexandria with a view of the U.S. Capitol dome. We celebrated the summer holidays — Memorial Day, July 4, and Labor Day at concerts on the Capitol lawn. For six years, I held credentials to the House and Senate press galleries and five times witnessed State of the Union addresses in person, while Brett watched on television. Together — and with me pregnant with Henry — we watched President Bill Clinton be inaugurated in 1997. And in 1993, when the Statue of Freedom was set to be removed from the top of the dome for cleaning and restoration, Brett and I arrived before dawn with coffee in hand to watch a helicopter bring her down; only a few dozen were there. The Capitol meant so much to both of us, it seems somewhat fitting it would be the subject of our last conversation.

Text to Brett: January 6, 2021, 1:37 p.m.
Me: Seen the news? It is August 1991 in DC.

Brett: This will pass rapidly. Nobody likes a sore loser.

Me: I hope they don't shoot senators and congressmen.

Brett: I doubt it. I still believe in America.

Me: Are you watching? They breached the Capitol and up to Chamber doors, possibly.

Brett: Not watching. All will be well.

Me: It's history being made for sure.

Brett: Crazy. Also, for sure. Hillary warned us. The people didn't listen. Trump may have ruined Republicans. So it all goes. Got to play the long game. U.S. good. Soviet Union was bad. Good riddance and eventually Putin will go. US is engine for democracy and the world is trying to get on board. Optimistic for our children.

Me: I appreciate your long view.

Me: They have reported shots fired off the House floor.

By the time Brett and I traded messages again, five people had died, 138 Capitol police were injured but the trespassers removed. Senators and representatives were out of danger, and members of Congress resumed their official business of certifying the presidential election.

Text to Brett: January 6, 2021, 8:36 p.m.
Me: Really reminds me of August 1991.

Brett: On a more important matter, Landon has almost finished reading the book you gave him for Christmas. He has enjoyed reading 'Pax.' He likes having his own library.

My next messages came from Henry long after I was asleep.

Messenger: January 7, 2021
Henry (2:45 a.m.): The joint session is over. Biden and Harris were determined to have been elected.
Henry (3:29 a.m.): I'm not sure I'll be able to sleep.

CHAPTER **10**

It's Not the End of the World … Yet

The obvious advantage of having a sister who lives in Hawaii is that I have a free place to stay if and when I can manage the price of airfare to Hawaii. A less obvious advantage is that during sleepless pandemic nights, it was five hours earlier in Hawaii, and Peggy was awake.

Messenger: January 11, 2020, 11:59 p.m.
Me: Awake at midnight. My latest freak-out: being worried I will stop breathing in my sleep. The past few nights I have worried about this because it feels like as soon as I relax, my breathing slows and then my body wakes up.

Peggy: But have you stopped breathing the past few nights?

Me: I show plenty of signs during the day of being healthy. I haven't died but I often wake feeling shaky and anxious.

Me: It's normal to be out of your mind anxious when people and cats die, you're awaiting biopsy results and the nation teeters on the brink of civil war, right? …

That day ABC News reported it had obtained an internal FBI bulletin that said armed protests were being planned in all 50 state capitals and at the U.S. Capitol between then and inauguration day. According to ABC News: "The FBI has also received information in recent days on a group calling for 'storming' state, local and federal government courthouses and administrative buildings in the event President Donald Trump is removed from office prior to Inauguration Day." The newly installed Democrat-controlled Congress planned to vote on articles of impeachment against Trump in the coming days, on a charge of inciting insurrection on January 6. "The group is also planning to 'storm' government offices in every state the day President-elect Joe Biden will be inaugurated, regardless of whether the states certified electoral votes for Biden or Trump," the news reported.

Peggy: You can't control Washington. You can't control cats getting sick. You can't control biopsy results. …You definitely can't control if you stop breathing while asleep. Unless you don't sleep. Which isn't a really good plan.

Me: No disagreement there.

Peggy: How would you feel if you try the opposite? Accept your utter lack of control.

Me: You mean believe in God?

Peggy: No need to have anything else in control either. The acceptance of your inability to control all things we just listed is the most calming thing imaginable.

Me: Hmm. That feels like surrendering to death.

Peggy: So you actually feel you can control any of the things you just listed?

Me: I feel like I am supposed to.

Peggy: Ah, and who made you so powerful?

Me: Dad thought he could control whether we had nuclear war. So, Dad?

Peggy: Was he right?

Me: Jury is out. LOL.

Peggy: Or just way too arrogant.

Me: Possibly.

Our father had once confided in me that if, upon his own death, he was given the opportunity to talk to God, he had questions — the first one being why God seemed to do such a poor job of managing life on Earth. Dad thought he could do better. He was being facetious when he said that, but only somewhat, in the way a man of faith who had seen too much suffering inevitably reacts to all that doesn't make sense, if one is to believe a compassionate God is in charge. Dad remained a man of faith, however. I was faltering.

———————— ▭ ————————

The next morning the phone rang with the news I had been waiting on for 26 days, since the doctor first raised the possibility of cancer. The nurse was brief and matter of fact, as though she had a long list of calls to make and I was just one more. She said my biopsy was normal, there was no sign of cancer, and the doctor would like to start me on hormone replacement therapy. Just. Like. That.

Messenger: January 12, 2021, 2:55 p.m.
Me: The biopsy is normal.

Peggy: That's it? No exclamation point? No smiley face? NOTHING?

Me: I posted about it on Facebook.

Peggy: I need you to REALLY REALLY REALLY absorb that this is GOOD NEWS. GOOD NEWS that is not to be taken lightly. HUGE, GOOD, AMAZING news.

She asked if we were going to celebrate. I said we might get chocolate shakes from McDonald's. She thought it deserved more. I was in no real mood to celebrate. I felt a sense of foreboding. I was relieved to not have cancer, of course, but nothing in me felt like I was safe.

The next day, the House of Representatives voted to impeach Trump by a vote of 232-197. Ten Republicans supported the impeachment. The Senate delayed action until February and the inauguration of Biden went off without incident. Widespread armed protests did not materialize.

Facebook: January 20, 2021
Maybe it's just me, but I feel about Biden being sworn in like I did after getting the call the biopsy is clear … struggling to be relieved, to believe the good news, unable because I've been bracing against bad news for so long … This past year, the collective trauma of 2020, that's not something you get over in a day, is it? 😬

There's no denying that once Biden was inaugurated, there was a revived sense of hope at our house. It was 2021 and vaccinations were underway. We might soon be free not only of the threat of disease, but the soul-crushing isolation of the pandemic. Health care providers received initial vaccinations in mid-December. Nursing and retirement home residents were next in line. Brett's mother received her first vaccination on January 9. No one was considered fully vaccinated until two weeks after the second dose, which was administered a month after the first. Brett, who had seen little of his mother during 2020, was looking forward to seeing her again in February. Roy's mother, who lived independently, would have to wait longer for a vaccine and family visits.

In Wichita, the rollout was moving at a glacial pace. The Sedgwick County health department announced it would begin making vaccines available January 22 to residents ages 90 and up. Rationing by age was being done because the county had a limited supply of vaccine, and the oldest people were considered the most vulnerable to dying from Covid-19.

My 23-year-old son looked at this and estimated an interminable wait until July for him to be able to see his girlfriend without social distancing requirements. Henry had asked if he could at least hug her. After doing some online research, I consented to hugging under the "Harvard protocols." Some expert at Harvard Medical School had concluded people could safely hug with limited risk so long as both were masked, faced away from one another, held their breath, kept it brief, and used hand sanitizer afterward.

No one outside my immediate family believed a young adult would agree to all this. What would seem weirdly obsessive to most people felt fairly reasonable to my son and I, with our OCD, though Henry frequently wondered if I wasn't exaggerating the threat to Roy's life. He was 65 and had some "preexisting conditions" including his weight that put him in a high-risk category. But Henry noted that Roy routinely lifted weights and biked 10 miles at a time; he did not seem particularly vulnerable.

Henry was determined to find a way to get the three of us vaccinated as soon as possible. And darned if he didn't find one.

On January 27, Henry sent me a link to the Hodgeman County website. The rural county in Western Kansas said it was scheduling anyone 65 or older with preexisting conditions and their "caregivers." It noted that one need not be a paid caregiver.

Messenger: January 27, 2021

Henry: This one looks promising. Not too, too far away. You could get a vaccine too under a plain reading of their guidelines. Would you like me to inquire on your behalf?

Me: No, but I will look into it.

I called and got a busy signal, so I submitted a contact form on the website to ask if they would consider vaccinating me and Roy. I presented myself as a caregiver — I certainly felt like my family's caregiver through the pandemic — but was careful not to exaggerate.

Henry: My insane plan is working!

Me: Why don't you think about what the liberalized family rules should be once Roy and I have two vaccines but before you are vaccinated. Interim steps.

Me: Like maybe you can hug three times.

Me: Kidding!

Henry: Ha. Ha. Ha.

While I waited to hear back, I started thinking about the down-side of driving three hours away to a sparsely populated county to get vaccinated.

Me: If we have a bad reaction, we're going to be a long way from emergency medical care.

Henry: It's not that far from Dodge City.

Me: But as long as they have epi pens, we should be okay.

Me: I'm starting to wonder if calling myself a caregiver is grossly dishonest. I certainly feel like the household caregiver. But it's not like he has dementia.

Henry: I just need to give Roy a sponge bath, and I can get the vaccine too!

The next morning I received a reply from the Hodgeman County Public Health Department.

Messenger: January 28, 2021
Me: The good public health servants of Hodgeman County Kansas are welcoming us with the vaccine on February 4 at noon!

Henry: Incredible.

Henry: You didn't try to squeeze me in as "with enough pie I could be obese by then"?

Me: No, but when we go, I will ask if when we come for our second dose, if you can get your first. I didn't push because she said she had exactly two slots open for 65+ and caregiver.

Henry: Couldn't hurt to ask I suppose.

Henry: They understand you're not like a home health aide, right?

Me: Yes, I made it clear I am his wife. I didn't overstate anything.

Henry: Okay. Of course you were honest.

Henry: I am still in disbelief.

Roy was thrilled when I told him we were scheduled to get vaccinated the following week. Then he asked the question I had not thought to ask: How did Henry find Hodgeman County?

Henry, it seems, had applied his deep knowledge of math, politics, and voting trends. His hunt started after he read a news article indicating all counties were receiving minimum weekly shipments of 100 doses. He then started looking for the most sparsely populated counties, where the minimum shipment would stretch the farthest. These rural counties also strongly supported Trump. Trump voters, as a rule, were calling Covid-19 a hoax and resisting masks. Henry reasoned they would not be interested in the vaccine, and it turns out Henry was right.

With fewer than 2,000 residents, Hodgeman County ranks 101st most populated out of 105 Kansas counties. Of the 1,045 voters in the presidential election, 875 backed Trump. I found a news article from a week after the 2020 election that said Hodgeman County residents were refusing to cooperate with public health workers attempting to do contact tracing on those who tested positive. The atmosphere was so bad the previous county health director resigned in September.

For the first time, I saw an upside to the recalcitrance of Trump supporters. Their lack of interest in vaccination meant Roy and I could be vaccinated within a week — and safe from Covid-19 by St. Patrick's Day. Hodgeman County told us if the weather was bad on February 4, not to worry, we could reschedule a week or two later. I did not imagine anything could keep us from getting vaccinated. I was wrong. ❖

CHAPTER **11**

Afraid
of the Wrong Things

Was I always Apocalyptic Polly? I once felt the invincibility of youth. I had a safe if not entirely happy childhood. I was loved unconditionally by my parents, which emboldened me to risk not being loved by everyone else. I found my voice early and was praised for my courage to say unpopular things.

But I inherited anxiety and fear from my parents. Ignorance is bliss, but they never allowed me to be ignorant. My parents were deeply informed on most subjects and passed along every government health and safety warning and every lesson from the newspapers or "60 Minutes" detailing a lapse in judgment that led to someone's demise. I was never shielded from adult problems. For as long as I could remember, I knew about the things that threatened to kill us all. Nuclear war topped the list.

The Cuban Missile Crisis occurred five years before I was born, and I grew up hearing stories about how my father, a scientific adviser to two administrations, had been on the short list of people designated to shelter in a government bunker in West Virginia in the event of a nuclear attack. Dad would help rebuild the country, I was told, and the rest of us in the family were supposed to get along on our own.

The Cuban Missile Crisis was a turning point for my father, Dr. Bennett L. Basore. He was a "rocket scientist," which is to say he had been designing nuclear weapon delivery systems in 1962. He felt a part of the problem when he wanted to be part of a solution, so he jumped at the chance to take a job in the Kennedy Administration, working on arms control.

Dad helped develop the "Hot Line," a network of secured communication using teletype machines intended to alert the Soviets of an accidental nuclear launch as a way to avert all-out war. He applied his expertise in information theory to assess the true threat versus the perceived threat of each side's nuclear arms buildup. And he devised workable ways to assess whether the Soviets were complying with nuclear tests bans — one of which involved monitoring the dead grass patterns created by dried cow manure displaced by seismic activity.

All of this occurred before I was born in 1967, before Dad left full-time government work to become an engineering professor in my hometown of Stillwater, Oklahoma. But it meant that the threat of nuclear annihilation was dinner table conversation as I was growing up.

Somehow, though, Dad's mere existence made me feel safe. (Mom's too.) Growing up in Oklahoma, tornadoes were a regular threat. We had the basement, which made me feel safe. But more than that, I always had the knowledge that my Dad was literally watching out for me — and everyone else. As an amateur radio operator with Civil Defense, he and others like him would park on hilltops and survey the sky to report any cloud rotation that threatened to spawn a killer tornado. They would radio this in to the weather stations, which would issue warnings through the TV. I could hear their voices on the ham radio in our house.

I remember vividly the first time I went to Dad for reassurance and he couldn't provide it. It was August 19, 1991, and I was watching a coup unfold in the Soviet Union on television. I had been there just weeks before working as reporter. My then-husband, Brett, was still there. I called Dad with my fears, as I had countless times before. I was worried that Brett would die. Dad was straight with me, as he really had always been. "Well, I don't know that there's ever been a bloodless revolution in Russia before ..." Brett, of course, did come home safely. There was minimal violence and only a handful of casualties. But from then on, I began to feel more vulnerable.

In 1994, I miscarried my first pregnancy and felt the most unspeakable kind of grief, paralyzing to the point I required a year of pregnancy loss counseling before I could try again for a baby. (Henry was born in 1997.) In 2001, my father died suddenly of heatstroke just two months before the Twin Towers in New York City collapsed on September 11 on live TV. I grieved my loss as the nation grieved the 2,996 killed on 9-11. The next year, my mom died within two months of sharing her bladder cancer diagnosis. My brother, Paul, summed it up when I asked him how it felt for him that Mom was dead: "I've lost the thing that made me feel safe."

Losing my parents changed me. I became terrified of who I would lose next. Would it be my son, Henry? Would it be Roy, whom I had loved long before I married him? I spent the next 20 years in fear, no doubt instilling fear in my son, as I constantly pointed out dangers and urged caution:

- *Don't leave candles unattended or you will burn the house down.*

- *Don't leave meat to thaw on the counter, eat raw cookie*

79

dough, or cross-contaminate cutting boards or you will get salmonella.

- *Don't eat food left in the fridge three days or you will get food poisoning.*

- *Don't give aspirin to a child with a fever or they will get Reye's Syndrome.*

- *Don't drive late at night because the streets fill with drunken drivers after the bars close.*

- *Don't go to clubs, you could get shot or raped, or killed by a drunken driver coming home.*

- *Don't drive into floodwater or you could drown.*

- *Don't shower during a thunderstorm or you could get electrocuted. Get inside if you hear thunder even if you don't yet see lightning.*

- *Don't park on a hill without a parking brake or your car could roll downhill and crush someone.*

- *Don't use beverage containers made of glass while driving or you could get lacerated by broken glass in a car crash.*

- *Leave plenty of space between you and the car in front when driving so you don't get crushed to death if you are rear-ended.*

- *When turning left, keep your wheel straight while in the turn lane so if you get rear-ended you don't get pushed into oncoming traffic.*

- *Don't mow the yard in sandals or you could lose a toe.*

- *Don't negotiate with terrorists. (I'm not sure why. It's just bad.)*

- *Don't pay blackmailers, they will just keep coming back for more.*

- *Don't eat tuna fish while pregnant or mercury could harm the baby.*

- *Don't lift anything heavy while pregnant, you could miscarry.*

- *Don't clean cat boxes while pregnant, or toxoplasmosis could kill the baby.*

- *Don't let your baby sleep on his tummy or he could die of Sudden Infant Death Syndrome.*

- *Don't use a gas stove; choose electric so you don't get carbon monoxide poisoning.*

- *Don't use white paper coffee filters or you will get dioxin poisoning.*

- *Don't over-exert in the heat and humidity or you will get heatstroke.*

- *Don't stay out too long in the cold or you will get frostbite.*

- *Don't talk to strangers. Avoid white panel vans. Don't accept anything but wrapped candy at Halloween.*

- *Don't shoot fireworks while your face is over the launch tube, without water nearby, or during periods of drought, or you will blow your face off or start a fire. (Better yet, don't shoot fireworks.)*

- *Don't smoke or you will get cancer. Don't get too many X-rays or you will get cancer. Don't take too many airplane flights because high-altitude radiation can give you cancer.*

- *Don't take medication from unsealed bottles. Don't take more than prescribed. Don't take less. Don't drink booze if you take medication.*

- *Absolutely don't use recreational drugs. They can give you a heart attack, or hallucinations in five years that make you want to jump off a roof.*

- *Don't have guns in the house; they are far more likely to be used in a suicide than shooting an intruder.*
- *Look both ways before crossing a street, use turn signals, and read the fine print.*
- *Black mold can kill you. Radon can kill you. Carbon monoxide can kill you. Donuts can kill you — but all things in moderation, including moderation.*

Is it any wonder Brett called me Apocalyptic Polly? Is it any surprise I readily complied during a global pandemic with instructions to wash my hands, not touch my face, wear a mask, stay home, or stand 6 feet apart, and get vaccinated? Yet none of that caution, absolutely none of it, protected me from what was coming. ❖

CHAPTER 12

They Are Out
of Beef Stew

It was Groundhog Day 2021 when I watched Roy nearly die on the floor of our kitchen.

It was up until that point, a pandemic day like any other, except for the fact it was the first day of the spring semester at the university, which had delayed its start until February. The three of us discussed the political news, watched the Covid-19 numbers climb, went about our home routine, and ordered Jason's Deli from Door-Dash.

Roy was in the kitchen cleaning up the takeout trash when I heard him call out with a seriousness and urgency I had never heard before — and I have known him since 1998: *"Polly, call 911! I am having a pulmonary embolism!"*

He hit the floor kitchen immediately after that, and I forgot how to dial the phone. Adrenaline hit my heart and the rush nearly blanked my mind. I dialed 911, then wondered why the call didn't connect. I had forgotten to hit the call button. I dialed again, hit "call" and waited. I don't have a clear memory of what happened next, just some scenes the trauma of the moment didn't steal.

I remember Roy on his knees in the kitchen, wheezing and panting loudly. I remember me on the porch, trying to read the numbers on the house to the 911 dispatcher so I didn't get them wrong. I remember Henry standing over Roy, saying he was still breathing but no longer conscious. I remember time stopping — or was it collapsing on itself? — as I stood on the porch listening for sirens and the promise of help on the way. I remember the ambulance and fire engine pulling up, paramedics rushing into our house, shoving the dining table and chairs out of the way, our dinner dishes tumbling into one another.

I stayed out of our small kitchen to give them room — or was it to avoid looking at the sight that terrified me? Henry stayed next to Roy, watching him turn gray. (I learned later his O_2 sats fell into the 60s.) I overheard a female paramedic ask Roy if he wanted "everything done" to save his life or not.

"Yes! Absolutely!" I called out from the next room.

"Ma'am. It's not your decision. It's his, as long as he can answer."

Roy wasn't answering.

"Do everything!" I said.

This was not my first DNR rodeo.

When my dad had heatstroke, he had been left brain dead. I knew he wanted to be allowed to die. I had no question. But it was not up to me, it was up to his wife, whom he had married just three weeks prior, the hopeful act of a 78-year-old man who thought he had at least 10 good years left. It took her nearly 24 hours to resign herself to the fact he was not coming back.

A few years later, it fell to me as the nearest living relative to sign a DNR allowing my Great Aunt Dorothy to die after she collapsed. I did not know her wishes, but my gut said to let her go. She started breathing again on her own and lived another year.

Roy was in and out of consciousness and seized as they put him on oxygen, moved him onto the stretcher, and carried him toward the ambulance. He was awake as I leaned over him in the front yard, kissed him on the forehead, and said what I thought was my last "I love you." I wondered how I would tell his children if he died. Henry and I stood in the yard and watched: The ambulance did not move. *Why was it not moving?* They had suggested taking him to the nearest hospital to be safe. *Why was it not moving? Was he already dead? Is that why?*

I remembered Roy's cell phone, ran in the house to retrieve it, and handed it to a paramedic not yet on the ambulance. I assumed that because of Covid-19, I would not be allowed to join him in the hospital. I asked Henry to drive me there anyway. While we were on the way, a paramedic used Roy's phone to call me and tell me he had stabilized, his color returned, and I could join him in the ER. They were surprised when I said, "Good. I'm in the parking lot."

———————— ▭ ————————

At 4:40 p.m., I was texting Henry about how Jason's Deli was out of beef stew, so I had to order him spicy seafood gumbo instead. My next message 2 hours and 15 minutes later — after Roy almost died in front of us — was about how it now looked like Roy would live. After dropping me at the ER, Henry waited outside in the parking lot. For hours. Due to Covid-19, he was not permitted inside.

> **Messenger:** February 2, 2021, 6:05 p.m.
> **Me:** Everyone here says he is better. I called Rose. She is calling everyone else. Do you mind staying out there for now?

> **Henry:** I don't mind

Messenger: February 2, 2021, 7:51 p.m.

Me: He's getting his ICU room, non-Covid ward. I'm allowed 15 minutes then need to leave. So not much longer.

Henry: Okay.

Me: Honestly, I want to go home. I want to clean everything, take a shower and collapse. In my bed, not the kitchen.

Henry: Good to clarify.

Me: I am sorry you missed your class. I will reschedule with Hodgeman County.

Henry: Okay. Hopefully you can.

Henry: How is Roy's breathing?

Me: Like nothing happened. It's kind of amazing.

Me: This is one of those traumatic things I hope I forget.

Messenger: February 2, 2021, 10:20 p.m.

Me: He had another breathing episode when he tried to stand up to pee.

Henry: Status?

Me: He's "fine" now.

Henry: His word?

Me: Yeah.

Me: I'm kind of at my limit for trying to stay calm. He's the one who calms me down when I have panic attacks.

Henry: You are not required to stay calm.

Me: I was so hopeful we would get vaccinated on Thursday and fear would recede from my life.

Me: The reason I go through life consumed with fear of something happening to my loved ones is I know disaster strikes on the most ordinary days. It is a hard thing to get over. I hope I can.

While Henry was texting me during his four-and-a-half-hour wait in the parking lot, he spent much of the time on the phone with his dad. I was glad Brett was able to keep him company after the trauma Henry had witnessed that evening. I was startled when Henry told me much later that Brett took real interest in the details about what had happened to Roy and wondered what it would be like to go through a cardiac event like that.

Walking around the ICU, I noticed something: Roy was the only one on the floor who wasn't on a ventilator. It was chilling to realize this, but it may explain why he was released less than 72 hours after admission. It was not immediately clear what had caused the blood clots that caused his pulmonary embolism. Covid-19 can cause clots, but he was tested and came back negative. His lungs were full of hundreds of clots. He was prescribed the blood-thinner Eliquis — for life, he was told — to reduce the clots.

Cancer can sometimes be an underlying cause of blood clotting. He underwent multiple CT scans and no tumors were found. His cardiologist scheduled him to meet with a hematologist to check for genetic conditions that might explain the clotting. He also scheduled to undergo a stress test in three months to check for a possible heart blockage. The EKG had not detected anything, but blood tests detected an enzyme suggesting possible heart damage. He was sent home with supplemental oxygen. Doctors in the hospital also encouraged him to get vaccinated as soon as possible.

Messenger: February 5, 2021, 10:25 a.m.

Me: The paramedic crew who saved him just stopped in to say hi. I almost cried. They were so happy to see him doing well. It was beautiful.

Henry: Yeah, I guess that's the really rewarding part of the job. They don't get to do that for everyone, of course. A tough job indeed.

Me: Roy thinks you now legitimately qualify as one of his caregivers and we should try to get you the vaccine too.

Me: You don't get to give him a sponge bath. He was pretty adamant about that. LOL.

Henry: Okay, I am good with that.

When I called Hodgeman County to cancel, they said it was fine to reschedule but they weren't sure when. They were no longer getting the same minimum 100 doses per week from the state. It seems the state decided it made more sense to give the smaller counties doses every other week so that more vaccine would go to large counties like ours. But our county was only vaccinating people ages 80 and up.

Facebook: February 5, 2021

Less than 72 hours since his collapse, Roy is back home. The oxygen machine is pumping away. He's resting on the sofa, saying how much better it is to be home. And I'm burning up Amazon Prime buying an electric shaver, a blood pressure cuff, etc. I am not quite as happy as him for him to be home, only because it feels too soon. It all feels too fast. He was in the hospital 8 days with his last PE. This time, just three. But I imagine it's a function of stressed hospitals needing space for the Covid patients, so we will do our part. He is fairly steady on his feet with the oxygen. One day at a time ... and sometimes, one hour.

When Roy came home, he was tethered to a portable oxygenator with a relatively short line leading to the cannula that fed oxygen into his nose. It was heavy, and it fell to me to push or carry it behind him. We were promised a set of oxygen tanks with 30 feet of line, enough for him to freely move about the upper level of our house. But Covid-19 had increased demand for oxygen, and we had to wait for someone else to give up their tanks to be delivered ours.

The first few days of caregiving were trying. Roy needed several medications at specific intervals and his O_2 saturation, pulse rate, and temperature recorded regularly. I kept a notebook and recorded everything. I already had an oximeter — the thing you clip on your finger to measure your oxygen saturation and pulse — along with a contactless thermometer. I purchased both early in the pandemic and did temperature checks on the family regularly because a cough with fever was an indicator of infection, and because sick people with falling O_2 levels often didn't recognize how low their levels were until it was dangerously late. Data was my defense.

> **Messenger (to Henry):** February 6, 2021, 10:36 a.m.
> I'm wearing myself out pretty good. Up three times to take him to the bathroom. He wanted up at 5 so I cooked a full breakfast, did all the dishes. Got him settled on the sofa and got myself a couple of hours of sleep. Then he wanted to go to his desk. Then he wanted to make himself coffee. (Pretty impressive.) Then he bathes. So pretty independent, but still a lot of extra work for me.

Roy tired quickly of needing an escort to the bathroom so he decided to go on his own without wearing his oxygen tube. I didn't like the idea, but I was exhausted from escorting him. He measured 97 O_2 before the trip and 91 after. That worried me. Conventional wisdom was anything below 94 merited a trip to the ER. But the doctors at the hospital said Roy needed to wear the oxygen until he could walk around without it falling below 90.

Meanwhile, extreme winter weather was moving in. We were warned to prepare for power outages. This, too, seemed to threaten our lives.

> **Facebook:** February 8, 2021
> Roy was given a loaner O_2 concentrator device to hold us through weekend. It has already shown itself to have a nonfunctioning battery, necessitating the purchase of a very long extension cord that allows him to move through the house (with me carrying machine behind) without power interruption. These are situations I'm sure have solutions that can be handled when you have time and means to prepare. But it's unsettling when one is tossed into new life challenges with no warning or training, as we are here on just Day 6 after Roy's pulmonary embolism. So I wonder, how many of us are there? People awake in the night worrying about this, as freezing rain threatens?

Roy's oxygen tanks — which did not need electricity to work — arrived the next day. It brought me both relief and more anxiety. I had a guy whose job was to deliver oxygen tanks to Covid-19 patients all day long entering my house.

> ### Facebook: February 9, 2021
>
> *For the second time since March 11, 2020, we let someone in our home that wasn't me, Roy or Henry. The first time was a plumber to spare our house from flooding. The second was today when we let the home health guy bring us our permanent oxygenator and emergency backup tanks. It has not escaped me that despite somewhat extreme cautions, Roy and I both faced life or death health scares. Mine not actual, thank God, but a month of tests looking for cancer. Roy's very real pulmonary embolism, which I won't detail because the memory haunts me. And yet here we are, no one in this house has had Covid at least. Knock on wood. Bring on the vaccines! Wishing all of you good health. 😊😷*
>
> *Edit: It's been brought to my attention I neglected to mention the team of paramedics last week that we welcomed in rather frantically. I guess that's how much I don't want to think about that — even as grateful to them that I am.*

All of this stress left my own body on a constant state of alert. My heart was racing. I felt stuck in the terrifying moment of making the 911 call, adrenaline shooting through my body. On a lark, I used the oximeter to check my own pulse. It was 110 bpm at rest. Tachycardia. Roy, meanwhile, was occasionally dipping below 50 bpm.

I went to see the doctor. He did an EKG to rule out actual heart problems, concluded my problem was anxiety, and placed me on a beta blocker, 25 mg of Metoprolol, to slow my heart rate. It did that — and more. I was suddenly incapacitated with weakness and nausea. I couldn't walk stairs, so I was cut off from the basement laundry and shower. I couldn't lift grocery bags, or really anything more than a dinner plate. I had no energy for doing dishes, which Roy had been doing by hand for a month since the dishwasher stopped working.

I felt overwhelmed by helplessness. Roy was doing more each day and Henry could help when asked, but he had also been traumatized by what happened to Roy, making his OCD and reluctance to touch things more pronounced. In the middle of the night, I went to Facebook to ask for help.

> **Facebook:** February 11, 2021
>
> *It's a blur now but I know when Roy first went in the hospital, several of you asked how you could help. I didn't know how to answer. I put everything into taking care of him and in the course of doing so, surfaced my own heart problem. I had an EKG on Monday and they put me on beta blockers, which I hear you adjust to, but right now, the drugs have made me nauseous and sapped my strength. ... This makes it hard to care for someone else. ... So if there is someone we know who wants to offer a bit of help — who is likely not to have or carry Covid due to vaccination and/or recent recovery — please DM me. Struggling here.*

People answered. Soon I was getting meals dropped off on my porch, deliveries from Walmart of disposable cups, plates, bowls, and utensils, and one friend vaccinated early as a health care provider came by to handwash dishes, run a vacuum, and do a load of laundry. Dozens more sent encouraging words. It helped.

Roy improved quickly. Another doctor weaned me off the beta blocker. I regained my strength but not the racing heart. Things were looking good — except for the weather. Climate change appeared ready to kill us again.

A shifting jet stream was bringing arctic cold, snow, sleet, freezing rain, and record low temperatures to much of the nation. The Polar Vortex, they called it. South Texas saw its palm fronds and tropical flowers killed off in subfreezing temperatures that overwhelmed their power grid and led to massive outages. On Facebook I watched as Texas friends for days relied on fireplaces for heat, bundling in coats and blankets against temps in their houses that fell into the 30s and 40s. Snow fell on Galveston Beach. In Kansas, we saw snow and a low of -12 on February 16. I got to experience windchills of

-29 while feeding my outdoor cat, who refused to come in. Roy and I called up "Dr. Zhivago" on Netflix and hoped that our power wouldn't go out.

Messenger: February 15, 2021

Henry: Alexis is telling me everything we need in an emergency kit:
Solar charging battery packs
Heat blanket/cold pack
Antibiotics
Antiseptics
Wrappings
Bandages
Crank lamp
Crank radio
Emergency provisions
Water
Water cleaner
Water tester
Sterno Striker

Me: She's a survivor. I've seen those lists. We should have it. But right now, I need to not think like that. I discussed it with my therapist today.

Henry: Yeah. Don't mean to worry you. That lists looks like its oriented to hurricane preparedness anyway.

I was sure my last remaining cat would die, but she didn't. Noel had shelter in the detached garage and a heated cat bed, along with a bellyful of fat that dragged the ground, and a coat of fur so thick she resembled a small polar bear. When I posted a photo of her, a family member commented, *"I'm certainly not body shaming her, but she looks like she has some resources stored to keep her warm."* Indeed.

Somehow, we made it through without losing power. When I wanted to reassure myself we still had power, I looked toward the front room for the glow of lights still illuminated on the Christmas tree, 54 days after Christmas.

With warming temperatures, life was starting to look better. Roy's youngest daughter gave birth to her first child, a healthy baby girl, on February 19. My panic attacks were subsiding, Roy was still on oxygen but showing every sign of full recovery, and we successfully rescheduled our vaccine in Hodgeman County for March 1. I was finally starting to sleep at night.

The phone woke me at 12:36 a.m. on February 23. The caller ID said "Denise." Brett's sister. *Why would she be calling me after midnight?* ❖

CHAPTER 13

Apocalypse, Now

"If you are going to divorce me, why did we have Henry?"
It is late 1999 and Brett is holding Henry, a toddler, in his arms. I cannot believe he is asking this. It is the most painful moment to ever pass between us.

"Because Henry is the best thing to ever happen to us," I reply through tears, knowing that he knows this. That he will always know this.

I met Brett when I was 18 and married him when I was 21. We looked out over the horizon of time and planned our lives together. There were amazing adventures in New York City, Moscow, and Washington, D.C., before we moved to Kansas. But life did not go according to plan.

We wanted children. We lost our first child to miscarriage in 1994. After pregnancy loss counseling and fertility treatment, we had Henry in 1997. We both said Henry was the best thing that ever happened to us. And never have I met a man who loved being a father more.

After Henry was born, I continued to work as a journalist and Brett became a full-time dad. He thrived, and so did Henry. After I was laid off from my job in Washington, D.C., we moved briefly to upstate New York where I took a job at a tabloid. I hated it.

Apocalyptic Polly

Within the year, we moved again to Wichita, where I took a job at The Wichita Eagle and met Roy. The details of what happened next are not for this book. Suffice it to say, Brett and I divorced each other, but remained bonded through Henry.

We parented together as closely as if we had stayed under the same roof. Through phone calls and emails and text messages, we discussed Henry. Brett often thought I was too protective, worrying too much about things unlikely to happen. But the fact is, the only time I ever really relaxed was when Henry was with Brett and his family. I knew they loved him as much as I did and would sacrifice anything to protect him.

Brett was ever present in Henry's life, even after he moved to Tulsa when Henry was 6. Twice a month he came to Wichita and stayed several days. Brett and I sat next to each other at Henry's academic league competitions, choir concerts, band performances, track meets, swim meets, cross country meets, and award ceremonies. Henry's friends occasionally mistook us for married.

Brett was married to someone else. He re-met April at his 20th high school reunion in 2002. He married her in 2005. Our personalities were different. April, I thought, made a much better wife for Brett — but I would not fully appreciate her until the weeks following that phone call from Denise. That devastating phone call that changed everything.

Denise was trying to reach Henry in that after-midnight call. She had news. Her voice was steady and calm in that kind of way that signals what is coming is going to be very bad news, and it was. I used the same tone when I woke Henry up and asked him to come sit on the sofa so that we could call Denise and she could share her news with him. We sat down in the dark, the room softly illuminated by the ever-present Christmas tree.

Henry braced himself. He had received bad news before — just four years earlier — when his dad called to tell him he needed to come to Tulsa, his grandfather was dying. Henry thought this call was about his grandma. I knew it wasn't, but I was going to let Denise break the news:

Earlier in the evening, Brett had come in from a run. He was a runner most of his life. Running was his way of coping with stress. There had been a lot. Brett had just moved his wife, April, her mother Sandy, and their grandson, Landon, into a new house, large enough for all of them to live together. He did this in the middle of a pandemic, through the Polar Vortex. He'd been coughing for days.

When he came in from the run, he felt off. He sat on the bed in his bedroom with April. His eyes rolled back in his head, and he collapsed. April called to Sandy, her mother, and Landon to come help her get Brett off the bed and onto the floor to do CPR while they waited for an ambulance. The ambulance took 10 minutes to arrive. Brett had a massive heart attack and had gone into cardiac arrest. The good news was he made it to the hospital alive: At the hospital, he had emergency surgery to clear blockages in three arteries and have a stent placed. The bad news: He was now on a ventilator.

It's hard to explain how shocking this was. Brett seemed exceptionally fit. He'd been a state-champion high school football player, a one-time triathlete, all his life a runner, and late in life, a competitive swimmer. He ate a healthy, low cholesterol diet so bland and disciplined friends teased him for it. He took high blood pressure medication but showed no outward sign of heart problems.

Henry wanted to get in the car and go to his dad immediately. Denise said April said to wait. Brett was unconscious and due to Covid-19, no visitors at all were allowed in the hospital, though April was permitted to see him briefly after he first arrived.

Text message to Henry: February 24, 2021, around 2 a.m.
April: I just got done seeing him and he was trying to raise up and they had to sedate him but I could tell he could hear me telling him to relax and lay down and everything was going to be alright but he had to rest and get better. Love you and your Dad. He will get through this.

I had a premonition early in the pandemic that Brett was going to die, but I wrote it off to anxiety, perhaps triggered by Brett's own speculation that he might not see his birthday in 2020. But the truth was, whenever I looked out over the horizon of life, I had imagined many people dying, but never Brett. I always expected him to be there, loving Henry with me.

I wasn't sure I believed in the power of prayer. I certainly didn't believe God blessed some and punished others based on what they deserved. But I embraced Pascal's Wager and went to Facebook and asked people to pray. I began regular updates on Brett's condition.

Facebook: February 24, 2021
The cardiologist told Brett's wife today that he's made more progress in 48 hours than some make in 30 days. 😊 *He is still critical, but stable, on a ventilator, with a pump supporting his heart. And he's being treated with antibiotics for pneumonia that they believe he may have had before the heart attack. But he is stabilizing, requiring fewer drugs to support his vital signs, and shows good function in all other organs. He is responsive and would be conscious if not for sedatives being used to prevent him dislodging the breathing tube. Doctors may remove the pump supporting his heart function tomorrow. That has to happen before he can come off ventilator. We are hopeful. Please keep lifting him up.* ♥

While Brett lay alone in a hospital room on a ventilator, my mind kept taking me to May 1991. We were living in a New York City apartment building on Riverside Boulevard, married student housing for Columbia University where I had just graduated. We were getting ready to go to Moscow, where I had gotten an internship at an English-language newspaper. I was a child of the Cold War and going to Moscow to be a reporter was my dream. Brett had been to the Soviet Union twice already and knew we would need to take most of what we needed because little would be available to buy there. The country was on the brink of economic collapse. We had a giant duffel bag his mom had purchased us. We stuffed it full of clothes and books and pots and pans and peanut butter jars and a water filter and who knows what else. I looked at it and worried. *"There's no way you can carry that. It's too heavy. There's no way."* And then Brett did one of the most Brett things ever: He took me and the duffel bag to the elevator, and we went down from our 3rd floor apartment to the 1st floor of the building. And then Brett slung that duffel bag on his shoulder and started to climb the stairs. Five flights up. Five flights down. Then he did it again. He looked at me defiantly. *"There. Convinced?"* The bag strap left a bruise mark on his shoulder, but I no longer argued.

I reminded Brett of this as a nurse held an iPad allowing Henry and I to video call him while he lay immobilized in the hospital. *"Remember how you did that? If you did that, you can do this. Henry and Landon need you to do this. Fight. Come on, you can do this."* Henry sat next to me and brought me back to earth. *"Mom, what if he can't do it? Then you're just shaming him."* Ouch.

The man I saw lying unconscious on a ventilator looked like nothing the man I had known for 35 years. Or rather, he looked in a state I knew he would never want to be. Henry knew it, too. I suddenly imagined Brett there with us, sitting beside me. In the image my mind projected, he looked like he did in 1991. Strong and invincible, defiant and angry. *"Man, this is bullshit. What is this?"* He was shouting at the image of himself on the iPad. *"What is this shit?! I don't want this. I never wanted this!"*

Brett had majored in philosophy — it was a main reason I married him. He got a master's degree in Russian literature. He had spent his life studying the great philosophers and writers, thinking about life and what it meant, and death. On December 31, 2020, I had texted him a New Year's greeting with a funny meme that said, *"Existence is a scam made up by philosophers to sell more philosophy."* He replied, *"Or as Dr. Lawry expressed, it all boils down to two things: piss and shit."*

He thought and spoke more about life and death than anyone I had ever known. I began rereading old emails from him and found this from February 26, 2019: *"Tough this life. Nobody can explain it and there is no manual."* We were having yet another conversation about Henry, and Brett was saying how hard he was trying to help Henry, and Landon and Landon's mother, Paige, his stepdaughter. *"As I approach the end of my own life, I would like to say that I helped the people most precious to me succeed."* He went on, projecting from his own experience as a stepparent to Roy's. *"A special thanks to Roy for helping Henry. There is a special place for him and me, for helping sons that are not our own. I promise Roy that Henry is worth all he has put into him. I know Landon is worth everything I have devoted to him."*

Brett knew about life, and I knew how he didn't want to die. But it wasn't up to me. And at first, we still had hope.

Even Henry at age 23 already had experience with a loved one in the hospital, dying. When he got that call from his dad four years before to come to Tulsa, Henry joined his extended family in the hospital room with his grandfather.

Brett's dad had collapsed at work, unable to breathe. He had idiopathic pulmonary fibrosis and knew the end was near, so much so that he'd prearranged his funeral. Together, Henry and his dad and grandma and others sat, reading over the will for direction on what to do.

Henry told the others that there was no question Poppie, as he was known, did not want to remain on life support. They let him go the next day. Henry had called me from that hospital room, several times. He knew I had been through this myself with my own father.

In 2001, I received a call at work from my stepmother, Linda, that Dad had collapsed from heatstroke while cleaning out a storage unit. It was 140 degrees inside the unit. Roy drove me to Stillwater. He waited in the waiting room while I stayed next to Dad holding his hand as he lay brain dead. In the hospital room with me were Linda, his wife, her daughters, and later Peggy, who flew in from Atlanta. We kept in touch by phone with my brother, Paul, living then in Australia. Just as I had felt Brett telling me he wanted to go, I had felt my dad saying the same. Linda found the strength by the next day and we were all together for the end.

A year later in 2002, after my mom was diagnosed with cancer, I was not at her side at the end. She died at home in hospice. But I had spent days at her side in the hospital and in hospice, with my sister. Paul had flown out to be with her, too. While our mother died, we had the comfort of each other.

This is how it is done, how it is supposed to be done. But not with Covid-19. The pandemic stole from us every gathering ritual that had ever brought a family comfort. Hospitals denied visitors. Waiting rooms were closed off with tape. Everything intended to reduce the spread of Covid instead spread pain.

Henry and I waited every day to get a report on Brett's condition from the hospital. Doctors would call April, then she would call us. Occasionally Henry would call the floor nurse, but someone shut that down and said no more calls allowed. The nursing staff had too much to do to take calls from more than one person per family.

The wait for the daily update was excruciating. We could barely eat dinner because the call usually came around 6 p.m. When it came, Henry would take it on speaker phone, lying in bed in his room, in the dark, me sitting on the floor. We hung on every word. I taught Henry in times like these when you call someone with such news, always open with "he's not dead," if that is indeed true.

Brett would have smirked at the absurdity of it all. In what other circumstance would you have a loved one on a ventilator and not have family together in the same room, at the hospital, supporting each other? Even Grandma who had been vaccinated in January couldn't go to the side of her son.

You could have stabbed me with a jagged knife and pulled it through my flesh and it would not have hurt worse. How had I been so fortunate to be allowed to be with Roy? I suddenly wondered what it was like for Roy's ex-wife to not be there when Roy was hospitalized. It was all too much.

Henry wanted to go to Tulsa, if only to be with Grandma and April and Landon. Even if he couldn't see his dad. But there was a problem. None of us were vaccinated, except for Grandma, and her assisted living center was still keeping residents in lockdown.

April didn't want to take a chance with her mother being exposed. And we didn't want to risk bringing Covid back home to Roy. We considered Henry going anyway, staying in a hotel and not with April, then isolating in the basement on his return, if needed. April said no. She called me, "You are his mother. He needs you. He can't get in to see his dad and he does not need to be staying here alone."

She made sense. She was strong. I found myself wondering about this woman who had been married to my (first) husband these past 20 years that I realized I didn't know at all. I found myself incredibly grateful for her. I had known she and Henry had a relationship, but I had never really witnessed it before. It was obvious now. They loved each other. I was grateful for that, too.

Facebook: February 28, 2021

Update on Henry's Dad: Better news today. Still on a ventilator but conscious, communicating with doctors through nodding, vitals steady and good. His wife got to see him through FaceTime. His heart is doing much better; we need his lungs to do the same so we can get him off the ventilator safely. Please keep lifting him up.

Facebook: March 3, 2021

Brett's condition is roughly the same, but I've been assured not getting worse is getting better. So keep those prayers coming for his lungs to heal so he can come off the ventilator.

Facebook: March 4, 2021

Not gonna sugarcoat it: Henry's dad, Brett, needs every ounce of healing energy the universe can send his way. Yesterday's report was disappointing: he has fluid in his lungs including blood from an unknown source, and until it clears the ventilator can't come out. The promising news is that his heart seems much better and it's his lungs that are limiting his ability to come off sedation and have the tubes removed. We are coming to terms that this could be a long wait for recovery, marked by ups and downs, and thanks to Covid preventing visitors, an almost unbearable wait on information from once-a-day updates. Please pray for our stamina and help us sustain hope. Thank you.

Facebook: March 10, 2021

Fourteen days since Henry's dad, Brett, went into cardiac arrest following a massive heart attack and was placed on a ventilator. Fourteen days of both loved ones and strangers praying for his recovery. Fourteen days of enduring this at a distance, Henry separated from his Dad's family; Brett separated from all but the medical personnel at the hospital. Every day he survives is cause for hope, but every day he remains on a ventilator because his lungs aren't well enough for him to come off ... it chips away at us. Trying to maintain anything of a normal life is nearly impossible, yet no alternative exists to simply enduring. I say this knowing how many of you have faced down cruel unexpected losses and grief in this past pandemic year, and before. Life is not a journey for the faint-hearted. Thank you to all who walk alongside us. ♥

Fourteen days on a ventilator. Friends in health care were telling me that was not a good sign. The lungs can only take so much. Fourteen days was a critical juncture where either care would be elevated or families would withdraw life support. That evening I got a text from Denise that said, "April has something she wants to tell us." *Oh shit!* I screamed.

I got Henry from his room and said to wait on the conference call that was coming. Turned out it was not THAT call. But the news was a lot to take in: Brett's lungs were failing, still full of fluid despite attempts to drain it. So the decision was made to transfer him that evening to a Tulsa heart hospital to be placed on a ECMO machine. Extracorporeal Membrane Oxygenation. The most aggressive treatment possible.

I briefly flashed back to Henry telling me, when I wondered if I might have cancer, *"Don't worry Mom. There are layers and layers of modern medicine between you and death."* Between Dad and death, now. ECMO survival rates were 60 percent. There was some room for hope. The machines were only supporting his lungs. Brett's heart was pumping the blood.

> **Facebook:** March 11, 2021
>
> *Significant update tonight.*
>
> *Henry's Dad, Brett, was transferred to the Oklahoma Heart Institute in Tulsa and placed on an ECMO machine, one of only three hospitals in the state to have this. This is state of the art tech that takes over the oxygenation and circulation of blood to let a body's heart and lungs heal. This is both good and bad; bad in that this is the last possible treatment to help him recover; good in that it's miraculous the machine was available and doctors thought him in good enough condition to be allocated this precious resource. Henry and I are in shock trying to process this. Please continue praying. It's all we have — that and the best technology 2021 provides.*

The change in hospital was significant in another way: This hospital would allow one visitor per patient in the ECMO suite. Henry was eager to go. It had been 18 days since the fateful call from Denise. In that time, something else significant changed, too. Henry, Roy, and I had all received our first shot of vaccine.

On February 26, Sedgwick County announced they were now administering vaccine to anyone 65 and older. We called Hodgeman County and asked if Henry could have Roy's shot on March 1. The good public health servants of Hodgeman County said yes. So the three of us made the six-hour round trip together, Roy's oxygen tanks in tow, so Henry and I could get vaccinated. Roy then got his vaccine in Wichita on March 2.

> **Messenger:** March 12, 2021
>
> **Me:** I am so excited April gets to see him. That means maybe you can too at some point.
>
> **Henry:** Yeah. I'll follow-up about the rules. "Some point" could be sooner than later.
>
> **Me:** I understand.
>
> **Henry:** I would really like to see him.
>
> **Me:** I am prepared to take you for a day trip. I think we could leave Roy alone for 48 hours. Or you can drive if you have a place to stay.

Later that day, Denise wrote to tell me she and her husband, Brent, were driving up from Austin, Texas, and that they would be glad to come to Wichita to get Henry to bring him to Tulsa. In other words, they were prepared to add six hours to an otherwise seven-hour trip. Denise and Brent were also more than two weeks out from their first dose of vaccine; Denise had both shots. In my restlessness of waiting for their arrival, I finally took down the Christmas tree.

April video-called us from the ECMO suite that night for about half an hour, showing us the equipment and updating us on Brett's condition. After he had been transferred, the nurses discovered the other hospital had never removed Brett's contacts. So his eyes were now open, red, puffy. He had always been so careful with his contacts. This was the kind of thing that got missed because no family was allowed in his room, I thought.

His pupils appeared different sizes. It was troubling. It could indicate a brain bleed — problematic because he was now on blood thinners for ECMO. CT scans did detect two small bleeds. There was discussion of an MRI to measure brain activity, but that couldn't be done so long as he was hooked to the equipment. Too much metal. His limbs were swollen from the fluid buildup in his body. He was no longer on paralytics or sedatives. We were waiting for him to wake up.

Text from April: March 13, 2021

April: I am with Brett, no change on cat scan from yesterday. They have had him off all sedation and pain medications since yesterday. We need him to wake up!

Me: They said yesterday it could be up to seven days for the sedation to leave his body. The fact that the CT scan doesn't show increased brain bleed is hugely good, I think.

April: Yes.

April: They are not going to change anything until they can access his brain. That is the focus first.

Me: I'm not sure you heard but Brent and Denise volunteered to come get Henry and take him to Tulsa tomorrow and stay at hotel with him …

April: Wow, lots of driving. Nice of them.

April: Henry needs to make sure he is appreciative out loud.

Messenger: March 13-14, 2021

10:11 p.m.
Me: Okay. April is up to speed. Landon is at a friend's house tonight so she can stay with Brett a long while. She is grateful for Brent driving you.

Henry: 👍

Me: I feel like maybe I can sleep tonight. I love knowing he's not alone. And you can go to Tulsa and not be alone.

6:34 a.m.
Henry: Some aggressive earthquakes.

7:09 a.m.
Me: Just now?

Henry: Like half an hour a go. Two in a row.

Me: I slept through it. Bad, by the looks on FB. Roy says he heard you exclaim.

We had earthquakes measuring 3.4? Of course we did. *Because the world is coming to an end.* A global pandemic. Hundreds of thousands dying of a deadly virus no one has natural immunity against. Hospitals under such strain that people who do get treatment get to die alone. Meanwhile across the nation, fires burn, floodwaters rise, beach towns freeze, democracy fights for survival, and people who should help each other snarl over whether to wear masks. It's fine. Just like the meme of the dog sitting in the burning house, we all tell ourselves: It's fine. If Brett did wake up, I know what he would say: "It's not like World War I. Now THAT was bad." That's what he always said whenever I, Apocalyptic Polly, ever worried about anything. I wished he would wake up and say it now.

On Sunday morning, we waited for Denise and Brent to come pick up Henry and take him to Tulsa. Roy sent me out to find a newspaper. In the days following Roy's pulmonary embolism, he went into reporter mode and began piecing together everything that happened that day I called 911 and the paramedic crew came and saved his life. He even got a recording of the 911 call. I couldn't listen to it. He transcribed it, tracked down everyone involved in saving his life, and wrote a story giving the typically unsung heroes their due.

He also confessed in the newspaper: *"I had felt funny for a month — and said nothing to Polly. Polly's a worrier. I dismiss her worries. I thought there was nothing wrong that more exercise couldn't fix."* He went on to describe what it felt like to be dead, or nearly: *"It's instant nothing. It is … void, an absence of moments and hours and seconds, an infinite, yawning Big Nothing deeper than sleep. If you are lucky enough to wake up from that place, it seems to you that you've been out for hours, not moments. In the realm of Nothing there are no words, no thoughts, no memories — no joys or regrets. There is only that tiny microsecond of awareness when you sense that time both stretches to the infinite and ends so abruptly that time never existed. And neither did you."* I put it together that his period of unconscious nothingness was when the paramedics were asking him whether he wanted everything done to save his life, telling me it wasn't my decision.

Facebook: March 15, 2021

By now many of you have read my husband Roy's gripping account of my nervous 911 call and the paramedics who answered and saved his life. Many readers remarked on the happy ending, one I'm profoundly grateful for on behalf of myself and Roy's children and family. But I cannot exhale the sigh of relief at a happy ending just yet.

Three weeks to the day after my husband had a pulmonary embolism my ex-husband had a massive heart attack and went into cardiac arrest as his wife had to call 911 as well. Their ambulance took 10 minutes, not four, during which time she and her mother gave Brett CPR. He survived to the hospital but was not sent home in three days like Roy.

Brett was on a ventilator for 14 days, then moved to a different hospital to be treated with ECMO, which oxygenates his blood through a machine to give his lungs a rest, where he remains. Brett's wife April endured 14 days of not being able to be at his side because of Covid rules, but thankfully she is permitted there at the second hospital. Throughout she has earned my profound respect for everything she has done starting with her 911 call and CPR to keep my son's father alive.

We learn a lot about what makes a family in times of crisis, and I can tell you with certainty it's not marriage or divorce. ... I definitely consider her family, much as I do Brett. Today Henry finally joins his Tulsa family to be together to await the outcome of Brett's story. We all want a happy ending — and yesterday there were some hopeful signs we might still get one.

But lives aren't made of happy endings. They are stitched together of day after day of uncertainty and struggle, punctuated, we hope, by moments of joy. The joy is in the love that comes and continues and is shared, no matter what. And that's what I am praying for, for Henry and his Tulsa family this week. The rest, as the song goes, is still unwritten.

On Monday morning, Henry headed straight to see his grandma first. Her assisted living center required him to take a rapid Covid-19 test. A year into the pandemic, this was his first test. It came back negative. And then got to hug his grandmother for the first time since January

Apocalyptic Polly

2020. She had been sick then, so sick Henry spent the night sleeping next to her in the event she needed help in the night. Grandma Judy, 80, had weathered cancer, strokes, heart attacks, and avoided Covid. She defied death with her resilient health. Now she was just sick of heart. Later that afternoon, he finally made it to the Tulsa heart hospital to be with Brett, his dad. Henry was dropped off, alone in the hospital. The medical attendant in the suite told Henry earlier on the phone that she had gotten Brett to blink, but he was otherwise unresponsive.

Messenger: March 15, 2021, 5:20 p.m.

Me: You ok?

Henry: Ha!

Henry: Good one.

Me: Sorry.

Me: Did you see him?

Henry: I'm with him now.

Me: Just you?

Henry: Yes.

Me: Tell him I love him and I wouldn't want anyone else to be your Dad.

Me: Please tell him that for me.

Henry: Done.

Henry stayed with Brett about an hour. Visitors are kicked out at 6:30. April planned to come back at 8 p.m. He squeezed his dad's hand, tried to get him to blink. Nothing. But he told me he thought Brett knew he was there. I peppered Henry with compulsive suggestions. *Play him R.E.M., anything from the "Murmur" album. Read him some Great American Speeches.* Brett read speeches to Henry as a baby. Henry meanwhile sent me links to articles about "Locked In Syndrome." He was growing increasingly afraid that his father was in there, but unable to move or communicate. The thought horrified him. His dad, the runner, one-time triathlete, late life swim competitor, writer, author, oral historian, father, husband, friend.

Messenger: March 15, 2021, 6:35 p.m.
Henry: Minimally conscious state also a strong contender.

Me: Did any medical person say this to you?

Henry: No. Just observing.

Me: You will make yourself crazy observing.

Henry: I saw up and down eye movement but no lateral.

Me: I understand the compulsion to want to identify and address the problem. But that's not for us to do using Google.

Later that night he picked up the phone and called me, pouring out his heart about the horrors of seeing his dad in such a state. He said the ECMO staff were matter of fact, not optimistic Brett would make it, and seemed to want to prepare Henry for the worst.

What does a mom tell her child at a time like this? Where is that super power that allows us to make them feel safe in the worst of circumstances? I thought of my dad being straight with me once I was adult that Brett in fact might not be okay. *Shit. Fuck. Goddamn it.* I told Henry it was going to be okay. One of two things was going to happen: He was going to wake up and get better and be part of our lives again. Or the family would make the decision to let him go. What would not happen, what would absolutely NOT happen, I assured Henry, is that Brett would stay in this horrific in-between state. This would end.

Messenger: March 16, 2021

12:31 a.m.
Me: Can't sleep?

Henry: Not yet.

Me: I hope you aren't doom-googling.

Henry: No.

Me: Good. Love you …

Henry: Love you too.

8:54 a.m.
Me: Did you sleep?

Henry: Yeah. Dreams of talking to my dad.

Henry did talk to his dad that day. He read Martin Luther King's "I Have a Dream" speech. He played R.E.M.'s "7 Chinese Brothers." He talked on and on, and sang, and sat silently, hoping for a response. At some point it all became too much and he made some gallows humor joke. That's when he thought he heard Brett laugh, a faint exhale that sounded to Henry like his father's laugh. When Henry told me, I had no doubt that Brett would laugh at the absurdity. I worried about Henry going all day dealing with the horrific sight of his father, his face and body distorted by the cumulative effects of his suffering, strapped to tubes and wires and a machine with blood flowing in and out of it. No one for company but medical people, who said the odds were not encouraging. But alone he was. The hours ticked down toward 6:30 p.m., when I knew Henry would be kicked out. I suddenly panicked. Time was running out.

6:15 p.m.
Me: Would you be willing to do a video call so I can see him?

Henry: Yes.

I got two minutes to say goodbye, my face visible to his, if indeed he could see, my voice where he could hear it. My mind flashed back to us at ages 21 and 25 on a hot August day, standing at the front of First Presbyterian Church in Stillwater, Oklahoma, holding hands and facing each other, Brett in a tuxedo and me in an ivory satin dress. Brett's nose was running from nervousness, but he smiled at me, that smile that assured me everything would be okay, even if we were scared. What should I say to Brett now in this moment? I did NOT say goodbye. I thanked him for being the ideal father to our son. And then I made him a promise, so that he would be at peace, if such a thing were possible: *Don't worry about Henry. I got this.*

Henry went back to the hotel and tried to process what he saw. He admitted to April that part of him wanted to take him off the machines now, while another part of him wondered, *"Hmm, could he be like Stephen Hawking and have a second act as a bed-bound intellectual?"* Around 10 p.m., he was summoned back to the hospital. Brett's whole family would go: his son, Henry, his wife, April, April's mom, Sandy, Brett's mom, Grandma Judy, his sister, Denise, and his Aunt Jan. The rule of one visitor no longer applied now. Just as the vet made an end-of-life exception, so did the doctors. A stent in Brett's heart had collapsed and his heart failed. There was no more hope of recovery. Just after midnight, the world ended. Or so it felt.

Facebook: March 17, 2021

As long as I have known him, Brett referred to life as a race, and death as a finishing line. He ran his race well and crossed the finish line early this morning. Our hearts are broken for the loss, but when his body suddenly gave out he spared his family a difficult choice. This man gave me the greatest gift I will ever have — my son, Henry — and I will always be grateful for the father he was, his decency and dedication to all his family and friends and everyone who knew him. Godspeed, my friend.

CHAPTER **14**

Death and How to Live with It

"Do we always adopt a cat when someone dies?"

Henry is asking me this less than a week after we buried his father. After the somber trip to J.C. Penney's to outfit him head to toe for the funeral. After the requisite trip to Super Cuts to get his unruly "Covid hair" and beard cut and shaved to please Grandma. After the painful moments I spent standing alone at the front of the Tulsa chapel, staring at Brett's casket in disbelief, wondering where Henry was, only to have him come to me in tears, his tie in disarray because no matter how many YouTube videos he watched in the bathroom, he couldn't tie it properly. Me, a mom fixing his tie now. A father's job, I thought, but no more father to do it.

"Yes, Henry. Yes, we do," I reply to his question about cats.

> **Messenger:** March 28, 2021, 10:21a.m.
> **Rose:** How are you?

> **Roy:** My house erupted in movement and excitement a few minutes ago. A microsecond after I told Polly yes, she could go get an 8-month-old rescued cat. I've never seen those two get dressed and go out the door so fast.

Henry was right. In his childhood there had been a lot of cats. In my life, a lot of death.

Heart-broken from my miscarriage in 1994, I persuaded Brett to let me adopt a sweet gray cat named Nelly, or more formally, Nelly Custis Kitty Cat, named for George Washington's stepdaughter because we lived near Washington, D.C.

I worried that Nelly was lonely, so the next year we adopted Buster, or more formally, George Washington Buster Custis. Gray and white, Buster had the lumbering manner of a basset hound. He was Henry's closest friend for many years. Brett got Nelly and Buster in the divorce.

In 2001, after my father died, I adopted Daisy, known as Wild Daisy, because the fearless white kitten insisted on leading an outdoor life of adventure. I didn't want her to be lonely either, so we also adopted Homer, named for the author of "The Iliad." Homer was an orange tabby polydactyl with six toes per foot, like Hemingway's cats, but he lacked Daisy's street smarts and go hit by a car while I was out of town, notably for a funeral.

My mom died soon after that in 2002. I adopted another orange tabby, Sunflower. He was my protector, killer of spiders in my bed as I slept.

In 2003, Brett told us he was moving home to Tulsa and would need to give his cats away. No way, I said, and welcomed Buster and Nelly back into my life.

In 2004, my Great Aunt Dorothy died. My sister and I had recently gone to the Bahamas using our inheritance from her. I came home and adopted a Siamese named Sandy, known formally as Sandy Bahama Beaches. Sandy had a bad habit of peeing on any fabric left on the floor, frequently including Henry's clothes, but also an endearing habit of coming to me at exactly 9 every night and meowing at me that it was time to come to bed.

Also in 2004, Simon died. Simon was a black and white stray who'd arrived in 2001, a streetwise cat who belonged to himself. He had many friends in our neighborhood and inspired the children's book I wrote about him called "Santa's Stray." He was found dead on Memorial Day. Neighbors came together to bury him in my yard. That same day, Tiger Lilly showed up. An emaciated calico who was too feral to live indoors, but she was a fierce survivor and I gave her a home.

In 2007, yet another stray showed up. He looked like walking roadkill. A desperately ill black longhair I named Midnight. I tried to save him, but he was diabetic and lasted only a few weeks. Shortly after, I adopted a black and white tuxedo kitten with white feet and named him Boots. When he grew too large to cuddle up under my chin, he became "Mr." Boots. He would be my companion for the next 13 years.

Buster died in 2009, then Nelly in 2010. That year, I adopted a tiny white kitten at Christmas and named her Noel, the one who would grow to resemble a small polar bear. A year into the pandemic, she was the only cat I had left. And I was worried she was lonely. I knew I was.

Days after Brett's funeral, I started searching pet adoption sites. A beautiful long-haired orange and yellow kitten caught my eye. She was a death row rescue named Twiglet. I wanted — perhaps too badly — to save someone from death. Henry and I rushed out of the house to go meet her. I had to fill out an application and come back the next day to see if I was approved. The next day I brought her home, my first new cat adoption in 11 years.

Roy, who had shown ambivalence about my cats, connected with Twiglet. He suggested she stay inside until she got used to her new home. We even left her inside when we made our second six-hour-roundtrip drive to Hodgeman County to get our second round of vaccine. She went out only a couple of times to explore the yard and so she and Noel could sniff each other.

We had a good few days together.

At first, we noticed she was napping quite a bit. Roy noticed she felt hot when he held her. Then we noticed the sneezing, drainage from the eyes. Within 48 hours she wasn't eating or drinking. It was April 4 — Easter and, God help us, Brett's birthday, the one he didn't make.

I was in denial about the cat. Roy's grandkids were coming over — he was two weeks out from his second vaccine and safe to see them. I made Easter dinner. Henry pressed me to get Twiglet checked out by a vet. There was no way I was going to say no. Not to my kid who lost his father less than a month ago.

Henry and I took Twiglet to the emergency vet clinic, open on Easter. The diagnosis was feline panleukopenia, a feline parvovirus. It was a kitten killer. Vaccines were supposed to protect against it but didn't always. I left Twiglet to stay at the hospital overnight. There wasn't zero chance of recovery, but it would require a long expensive hospitalization with low odds. The bill was already $1,400. I sobbed on the phone with the vet and told her I couldn't go through this again, not another series of days wondering if someone we loved would live or die. Not again.

Henry did not want to go this time. I held Twiglet — or was it Boots or was it Brett — and told her I loved her as I felt her life fade to nothing.

Messenger: April 5, 2021, 11:42 a.m.
Me: She's gone. 😿

Me: I held her in my arms throughout.

Henry: Understood.

Me: I love you.

Me: I am so sorry about everything.

Henry: Love you too. It's all just hard.

For weeks Henry and I had April 13 circled on the calendar. Something to look forward to: The day we would be fully vaccinated against the coronavirus. The day we would lift the family lockdown. The day he could date like a normal person. The day we would get our lives back.

Roy was a week ahead of us. He got vaccinated with Pfizer, which only required three weeks between shots; Moderna required four. Roy immediately went to see his daughter and granddaughters. Henry invited Alexis over for dinner. What did I look forward to most? Allowing repairmen in the house to replace the dishwasher and maids to help clean the house? I also scheduled my first hair appointment in over a year.

That didn't feel like enough. The three of us had just survived over a year of pandemic and all that came with it, death and near-death. What next? *Get a new dishwasher? Seriously?!*

Roy was not out of woods yet. The same day Twiglet died, Roy went for a CT screen at the cancer center to see if some hidden cancer had caused his blood clots. He got the all-clear on April 12. Now all that remained was a heart stress test scheduled for May to see if he had any blockages that needed to be dealt with. (He didn't).

Henry and I were more aware of what we didn't want to do than what we did. I knew it wasn't work. Henry knew it wasn't school. I decided to take two months of unpaid leave. Henry withdrew from all his classes. The day before I had adopted Twiglet I texted Henry:

> **Me:** I'm so confused about what I want from life right now. I know I want that cat. Funny huh? And time with you and Roy, and I want to write because I have a lot to write about. But that's all I got right now.

> **Henry:** Sounds like a fair amount of stuff.

Unable to envision our post-pandemic future, I focused instead on planning the next two weeks: Road trip! The three of us packed into the SUV and drove south to Texas. To Austin to see Brett's sister, Denise, and Roy's old friend Gary. To Galveston to see the beach — and palm trees still damaged by the freak freeze earlier in the year. To Houston to see NASA, museums, and friends. The first time we all went out to eat in a restaurant it felt a bit scary, but quickly liberating. The second time, it felt delightfully normal. As if the pandemic had never happened and we hadn't stayed at home, going nearly nowhere but to doctors and hospitals for more than a year.

It wasn't the greatest of vacations. Grief hung heavy over us; everything cost more than I felt it should have. And when we got home, both Roy and Henry got sick right away, then me a few weeks later. Not Covid-19 for any of us, but unnerving. But it was May now, and flowers in the backyard were blooming once again.

> **Facebook:** May 12, 2021
>
> *If I've learned anything about grief, it's that rituals matter. Mr. Boots died on Jan. 2. Today we finally got the sunshine combined with the iris garden in full blossom that I wanted to scatter his ashes there to say goodbye. These things help; I don't know why, but they do.*

The summer months were a blur. I returned to work in June, going into my office for the first time in 453 days. I was too numb to notice much going on in the outside world, other than the paradox of people refusing a vaccine we had tried so hard to get. By Labor Day 2021, just 62 percent of those eligible (ages 12+) were fully vaccinated. All kinds of efforts were put into getting shots to the rest, the "vaccine hesitant." The media was full of stories about people flat opposed to the vaccine — until they ended up on a ventilator.

Brett had not died a Covid-19 death, but his death closely resembled the Covid experience. The isolation in the hospital, weeks on the ventilator, failing lungs worn down by having air forced into them, a sci-fi ending on ECMO. I wondered how people were somehow choosing this. Because of their belief that Covid was a hoax and masks were a government plot of control and vaccinations were somehow a more frightening prospect? I vacillated between indifference and rage at their foolishness.

Henry pushed on, making monthly trips to Tulsa to see April and Landon, bringing home boxes of his Dad's things, me discovering my own past in many of them. *Oh! Here is that silver candelabra we got as a wedding gift, when the 20-something version of ourselves somehow imagined we might somehow need that one day.* I'm here to tell you 32 years later that we never did. I smiled at the discovery and put it in the garage with all the other things I couldn't let go of yet.

In May, Roy immersed himself in a new writing project that brought him out of retirement and back to life. He started riding his bike, wrecked it and then recovered, which helped me adjust to the idea that maybe he wouldn't die on me any time soon. I spent the spring and summer pursuing a job I thought I really wanted but didn't get, and confronted grief of another kind.

Henry pushed through 10 weeks of a remote internship with NASA. Many times Henry wondered if he would complete the internship or forever be known "as that intern who spilled coffee on the Challenger console." When he hit a point he could barely function, a kind soul at NASA asked if he had any quantum computing research he could "repurpose" for the internship. To my wonder, he did. I could feel Brett smiling from somewhere.

People asked me regularly how Henry was doing since Brett died. I gave my best answer in a post on Facebook, 20 years to the day after my own father died.

Facebook: July 7, 2021

My father's death from heatstroke 20 years ago today was a visceral horror that took long to recede to that place in the mind where you remember but no longer relive every moment of every day. I did remember again, of course, once my son went through something similar this year.

It was an ugly horrific end for Henry's father, drawn out through three weeks of life support, two of them spent in complete separation from his family, due to COVID restrictions; Henry was with him mostly alone over the final 48 hours, witnessing things it will take long to process.

His father died less than four months ago, so I am always startled by the frequent question: "How is Henry doing?" It's a well-intentioned question, but I am not sure what answer is expected.

How is he supposed to be doing? What are the developmental milestones for recovering from your father's unexpected death? Is this covered in a book called "What to Expect When You're Unsuspecting"?

The only benchmarks I have are my own, and they suggest that one is doing well simply by getting out of bed every day and not falling into habits of self-destruction.

In the wake of my father's death, followed the next year by my mother's, I outwardly appeared to function. Privately, I drank too much, spent too much, fell into deep depressions involving self-injury, and frequently balled up from unrelenting stomach pain. I suffered brain fog, lost short-term memory and struggled to find meaning in much of anything.

Two years into my grief, I became overwhelmed. I took leave from work, then impulsively quit my job, unaware I was also giving up my chosen career. Two decades hence I am still unsure if quitting was one of my worst mistakes, or simply a thing that needed to happen so other things could happen.

Facebook: July 7, 2021 (cont.)

In the third year of grief, I felt a sense of urgency to bring back my father by becoming him, or rather embodying the best of him. For me that took the form of philanthropy and public problem-solving, and that provided the purpose and meaning that eventually became my road out of despair.

Grief is not a thing to be worked through quickly, and the world doesn't always show the patience that is required. But the pain does lessen with time.

After 20 years, I no longer expect the phone to ring to hear Dad's voice. I no longer expect to see him pull his car into the drive. I no longer ache over what I cannot ask him. And that is in part because once I became accustomed to his physical absence, his lingering essence became more obvious.

He is ever present in my actions, my thoughts, my stories. Because we were blessed with being that close and having had countless conversations, I know in most cases what he would say in any given situations.

I tell this to my son, and I get some side eye. This does not get him answers to practical questions like "Where's the will, Dad?" and "What's the password to your laptop?" Fair enough. But I like to believe that in time, he will find the counsel of his father — and one day me — inside his heart.

A thing no one really teaches you in life — until death itself teaches you — is that you don't stop having a relationship with a person just because they die. The relationship, like the love, goes on. And when you finally realize that, it gets better, and the haunting memories no longer crowd out the joyous ones.

With money from NASA, some inheritance from his dad, and a new part-time job with a cybersecurity contractor, Henry moved out of our house and into a life of his own. His moving day was one day after my last day at work. With Roy's support, I left my salaried job to start writing, what exactly I did not yet know. I just knew I had to leave behind the life I'd lived during of the pandemic — and the deaths I witnessed — and begin anew.

I wasn't the only one. Millions of Americans voluntarily left jobs in 2021. Experts struggled for an explanation. NPR suggested in June 2021 people were seeking flexibility and meaning: "Many are rethinking what work means to them, how they are valued, and how they spend their time." We'd endured a collective trauma. Everything about normal life had changed. Major life disruption, we had been warned.

The pandemic wasn't over, of course. Cases were surging among the unvaccinated, straining hospitals once again. We were still being asked to wear masks, stay home when possible, and socially distance to reduce the spread of the virus. I did as I was asked to support public health measures, even if my own life was no longer at risk. That's how I was raised.

But this time, I did so in moderation. No more agoraphobia. I went out to eat. I went to movies. I met people for coffee and my therapist in person. I hugged family and friends. Roy and I taught our university class in person. I didn't argue when Roy wanted to travel the country for his project. I stopped worrying constantly about Henry.

I listened calmly when my son discussed his life plan to settle in Upper Peninsula Michigan, an area he concluded most likely to avoid the devastating effects of floods and fires brought on by climate change. I consoled myself that at least the threat of nuclear war would not hover over him, as it had me. Who could be sure, though? None of us.

We can prepare. We can try to prevent. And whatever happens, we must respond. But we need not be paralyzed by fear. I am no longer Apocalyptic Polly. Turns out, on the other side of the end of the world, I stopped being afraid of everything. Because I realized death is inevitable — and living well isn't.

❖ THE END ❖

Acknowledgments

Everyone who lived during 2020-21 has a pandemic story. This is my story — but not only my story.

I wish to acknowledge the people who lived through this with me and consented to have their words and experiences shared in this book: My son, Henry, my husband, Roy, Roy's daughter Rose, my sister, Peggy, my niece Melody, my ex-husband Brett's wife, April, and Brett's sister, Denise.

Thanks also to the team that brought this project to fruition: Brett's dear friend Brian Whepley for his editing and design work, Carlene Williams for executing my vision for the cover with her art, my former student Khristian Jones for her guidance on Chapter 4, and marketing maven Bonnie Tharp for believing in me when I needed it most.

Made in the USA
Coppell, TX
05 November 2021